SECRETS

of the

VINE

DEVOTIONAL

Bruce Wilkinson

with DAVID KOPP

Multnomah® Publishers *Sisters, Oregon*

SECRETS OF THE VINE DEVOTIONAL
published by Multnomah Publishers, Inc.
© 2002 by Bruce Wilkinson
International Standard Book Number: 1-57673-959-7

Cover design by David Carlson Design
Cover and interior illustrations by Katia Andreeva
© 2001 by Multnomah Publishers, Inc.

Scripture is from *The Holy Bible,* New King James Version.
Copyright © 1982 by Thomas Nelson, Inc. Used by permission.
Other Scripture quotations:
The Holy Bible, New International Version (NIV)
© 1973, 1984 by International Bible Society,
used by permission of Zondervan Publishing House

Multnomah is a trademark of Multnomah Publishers, Inc.,
and is registered in the U.S. Patent and Trademark Office.
The colophon is a trademark of Multnomah Publishers, Inc.
Printed in the United States of America

For information:
MULTNOMAH PUBLISHERS, INC.
POST OFFICE BOX 1720
SISTERS, OREGON 97759

02 03 04 05 06 07 08—10 9 8 7 6 5 4 3 2 1

ACKNOWLEDGMENTS

I'm grateful as always to David Kopp, my writing partner and editor, and to Heather
Harpham Kopp, our assisting editor, for the skill, dedication, and friendship both of
you bring to this ministry. My thanks goes also to Steffany Woolsey, David Webb,
Pamela McGrew, Judy Morrow, Michael Christopher, Ken Jones, Jeff Gerke, Galen
and Syndi Wright, Bill Mintiens, Penny Whipps, and Joel Kneedler. Your help and
support have been a gift from God.

—*Bruce Wilkinson*

CONTENTS

Week Three: Reaching for the Best

Week Four: Flourishing in His Presence

Epilogue: The Prize of Abundance

YOUR JOURNEY *to* ABUNDANCE

Everywhere I travel in the world, I meet people who are realizing that spiritual abundance is not only possible but expected of every believer—and they don't want to settle for less. After reading *Secrets of the Vine,* a woman named Sarena jotted me a note: "I don't have another day to waste," she said. "I want to be a passionate Christian. I want to have an overflowing basket for God."

Maybe you're like Sarena. You sense a deeper destiny, one that you may have missed for months or even years. But now you feel the breezes of the Spirit. Maybe you see a picture of the extraordinary abundance that God has in mind for you, and you want it with all your heart. If so, then the book you're holding is especially for you.

I wrote *Secrets of the Vine* to show how God works in our lives to bring us from barrenness to fruitfulness for His glory. The book is based on Jesus' teachings in a vineyard the night before He died (found in John 15). Using the illustrations of a vinedresser, a vine, a branch, and fruit, Jesus painted a memorable word picture of God's ways in our lives, what He wants most from us every day, and how we can cooperate with Him to make it happen. If you haven't read this little book yet, I urge you to do so.

The *Secrets of the Vine Devotional* will take you, step by step, further into the life you want—the one God wants even more for you. Here you'll find thirty-one days' worth of personal mentoring, encouragement, and practical suggestions for nurturing your spiritual transformation.

A companion tool, the *Secrets of the Vine Journal,* has been created especially for use with this devotional. If you haven't thought of yourself as a spiritual journaler before, I urge you to take this important step. At the conclusion of each day's reading you'll notice an entry called "My Vineyard Journal." These daily prompters suggest questions and prayers to enrich your journaling experience.

In your journal keeping, don't worry about *how* you write—just write. Make each page an ongoing conversation with God. Keep your entries personal, on task, and true. You are in an amazing season of your life. Don't miss a minute of it!

I recommend that you continue your exploration with the *Secrets of the Vine Bible Study* or the *Secrets of the Vine Video Series.* These studies work well for personal or group use and will take you deeper into the biblical truths and personal applications of spiritual abundance.

By the time you finish this devotional, you'll know what God has been doing in your life ever since you became a Christian. You'll grasp what it means to experience abundant fruitfulness for God. You'll begin to see more lasting results from your life than you ever thought possible—and you'll know for certain that even more are on the way.

Join me on this joyful, life-changing journey today.

—*Bruce Wilkinson*

I am the true vine, and My Father is the vinedresser.

Every branch in Me that does not bear fruit He takes away;

and every branch that bears fruit He prunes,

that it may bear more fruit.

I am the vine, you are the branches.

He who abides in Me, and I in him, bears much fruit;

for without Me you can do nothing.

By this is My Father is glorified, that you bear much fruit;

so you will be My disciples.

You did not choose Me, but I chose you and appointed you

that you should go and bear fruit,

and that your fruit should remain,

that whatever you ask the Father in My name

He may give you.

JOHN 15:1–2, 5, 8, 16

Week One

THE YIELD of YOUR LIFE

*"You did not choose Me,
but I chose you and appointed you that
you should go and bear fruit."*

JOHN 15:16

THE GREAT EXCHANGE

"If you keep My commandments, you will abide in My love,
just as I have kept My Father's commandments and abide in His love.
These things I have spoken to you, that My joy may remain in you,
and that your joy may be full."

JOHN 15:10–11

This is a book about grapes as a metaphor for supernatural abundance in your life. Big, beautiful, juicy grapes—bushels of them! But since I'm from Georgia, where we grow a lot of peaches, could I talk about peaches first?

One spring years ago, when our family first moved out to the country, I heard about a prize-winning local orchard. "Famous Georgia peaches," my neighbor said proudly, "big as melons, sweet as nectar." But the first time I saw the orchard, I was shocked. It was early spring, with not a peach in sight, and under every tree a thicket of long, unsightly poles propped up each branch.

Had a twister come through? Had some invisible disease attacked a once-famous landmark? I didn't know. I went home thinking it looked more like a tree hospital than a famous orchard.

When I asked my neighbor what had befallen the orchard, he

laughed. "Just wait a few months," he said. "You'll get the picture."

I went back to the orchard in midsummer…and I got the picture. The peaches were the largest, most beautiful I'd ever seen, and the crop was so heavy that the purpose of those poles became immediately clear. Without them, the sheer weight of ripening fruit would easily have snapped the branches.

As I walked through the rows of trees, I found myself praying. *Lord, may my life someday look like this orchard for You. May the fruit of my life be so heavy that You'll need angels to hold up the branches. And whatever You need to do in my life to make me a person who can produce that kind of abundance—Lord, please do it!*

That spontaneous prayer is at the heart of this little book—a plea for supernatural productivity for God's kingdom, and a plea for His work in our lives to make it possible.

These are requests God promises to answer. But there's a catch.

To get to the life God has in mind for you, you have to be willing to make an exchange. You have to be willing to go against the grain of what you may have assumed to be true, to be willing to respond to God in new ways that won't feel at all safe or smart, at least to begin with.

Bumper crops don't just naturally happen. So in this book, where our conversation is set in a vineyard, we'll be talking about things like mud and mildew, cleaning and restraining, and cutting away perfectly good growth. We'll also be talking about trying again in areas you may have tried hard in before.

But please don't hear the words and lose the picture. The words are about how God tends your life. The picture is what He's preparing you to produce—a harvest so extraordinary that you'll need His arms underneath you just to hold up your branch!

Are you willing to cooperate with how God works in your life at a deeper level? If so, then you are signing up for the great exchange. Jesus promised it to His disciples in the vineyard the last night He was alive. Jesus said you and I can expect to have this rarest abundance of all—an abundance of the heart—as we produce a harvest for Him. He said we can have it in full and should settle for nothing less.

He called it joy…. *These things I have spoken to you, that My joy may remain in you, and that your joy may be full.*

As you go through your day today, try this: Pull out all your old assumptions, worn-out expectations, and broken ideas about how God works in your life. Empty the junk drawers of your spirit.

Then find a moment to stand in the presence of Jesus and lay down your worthless collection. Tell Him it's time you made the great exchange. Accept His offer. And set out with me on the path toward a joy that remains.

MY VINEYARD JOURNAL: *"Lord, lead me into a life of extraordinary, joyful abundance for You. Help me to desire it passionately. Today, show me a glimpse of what my harvest could be like by this time next year."*

Joy comes from seeing the complete fulfillment of the specific purpose for which I was created and born again, not from successfully doing something of my own choosing.

OSWALD CHAMBERS

PICTURES *from the* VINEYARD

"I am the true vine, and My Father is the vinedresser.
I am the vine, you are the branches."

JOHN 15:1, 5

I f you've read *Secrets of the Vine,* you know that Jesus chose a
dramatic moment and a memorable word picture to tell His
best friends what they could expect in their future. The conversation
occurred only minutes after He had dashed all their hopes for earthly
glory and power (John 13, 14) and only hours before He was to be
crucified (John 19).

On their late-night walk from the upper room to Gethsemane,
Jesus had led His disciples into a vineyard outside the city walls.
There, Jesus paused. As torches flickered in the night air, His friends
waited. Perhaps they wondered what else remained to be said that
they could possibly want to hear.

But surrounded by carefully tended rows of grapes, Jesus began
a most surprising conversation.

"I am the true vine, and My Father is the vinedresser. Every
branch in Me that does not bear fruit He takes away; and every

branch that bears fruit He prunes, that it may bear more fruit. I am the vine, you are the branches. He who abides in Me, and I in him, bears much fruit.... By this My Father is glorified, that you bear much fruit. (John 15:1–2, 5, 8)

Think of how those words must have fallen on their ears. Instead of talk of legions of angels, Jesus talked about plants. Instead of insurrection, He spoke repeatedly of fruit bearing. And He told them that an ongoing relationship with Him was not only possible, but would be the key to producing more fruit.

Much more.

Notice how clearly Jesus identified what each part of the grape plant represented:

The vine is Jesus. The vine of the grape is the trunk that brings sap up from the roots into the branches.

The branches are His followers. Carefully tended branches grow out along trellises from both sides of the vine and produce the grapes.

The vineyard keeper is God the Father. The vinedresser in a vineyard has one purpose—to work on each branch individually so that it will bear the finest harvest of grapes.

The fruit is the good works of Jesus' disciples.

Are you beginning to see why Jesus left His friends with this picture of the vineyard? Here are several important truths from the vineyard that can change your life today:

1. *The vineyard shows you God's purpose for you.* Jesus wanted His followers to remember that we have one overarching purpose on earth—to bear fruit for God's glory.

2. *The vineyard shows that you have been created and are regularly being tended to succeed in this purpose.* The fact is, with the proper care, a grape branch is a wonder of the natural world—perfectly suited for exceptionally high crop yields year after year.

3. *The vineyard shows you how God will work in your life to achieve His purpose.* Clearly, the Father's activities in the vineyard are focused on increasing our output for Him. The Vinedresser is active, not passive; present, not absent; committed, not casual or careless.

4. *The vineyard shows that we are created for a living relationship with God.* Just as Jesus had earlier described Himself as the Good Shepherd, here He again chose an image that conveys a mysteriously interconnected relationship: The Vine gives its life to the branch; the ever present, ever involved Vinedresser tends the branch; the branch produces valuable fruit.

5. *The vineyard is proof that God wants you to be clear, not confused, about His ways in your life.* Unfortunately, many Christians misread His activities behind the scenes in their lives, and therefore slide into doubt and mistrust. Or they assume that real friendship with God is a spiritual accomplishment reserved for monks and missionaries.

But Jesus came to tell you and me the "secrets" of God at work in His vineyard. I encourage you to ask the Holy Spirit to open your heart to learn about fruitfulness today. And listen for the footsteps of your Father, the Vinedresser, in the rows of your life.

MY VINEYARD JOURNAL: *Up to now, what have I imagined Jesus wanted from my life? How might my thinking change, based on the truths Jesus revealed that night in the vineyard?*

Speak in my words today, think in my thoughts,
and work in all my deeds.
And seeing that it is Your gracious will
to make use even of such weak human instruments
in the fulfillment of Your mighty purpose for the world,
let my life today be the channel through
which some little portion of Your divine love
and pity may reach the lives that are nearest to my own.

JOHN BAILLIE

We do not look at the things which are seen,
but at the things which are not seen.
For the things which are seen are temporary,
but the things which are not seen are eternal.

2 CORINTHIANS 4:18

WHAT IS FRUIT?

And let our people also learn to maintain good works,
to meet urgent needs, that they may not be unfruitful.

TITUS 3:14

S omebody says banana, you think monkey. Somebody says apple,
you think homemade apple pie or maybe school lunch.

What do you think of when we talk about bearing fruit?

Fruit is God's picture of eternal results stemming from your life.
Paul's instruction to Titus in today's verse shows what the Bible
means when it talks about spiritual fruit. It's nearly synonymous with
good works. Biblically speaking, we could define fruit as a good work
that pleases God and that is done with an appropriate motive. In his
first letter, Peter exhorted the early Christians to live in such a way
that even hostile unbelievers would be persuaded to glorify God
when they saw their good works (1 Peter 2:11–12).

So fruit is the yield of your life. Fruit is leading others to the
Lord (John 4:35–38)—and it's much more. Fruit is teaching and
encouraging other believers (Romans 1:13). Fruit is helping or giving
(Philippians 4:16–17). Fruit is genuine worship (Hebrews 13:15).
Some include fruit as the beautiful outward expression of the inward

work of the Spirit in your character to make you more like Christ (Galatians 5:22–23; Colossians 1:3–8). Fruit, then, is any good work that brings glory to God (Titus 3:14).

The big difference between physical and spiritual fruit is that spiritual fruit blesses you now *and* lasts into eternity. Jesus invited His disciples to bear the fruit that would "remain" (John 15:16).

Yet even though you and I are chosen for just such productivity, our lives can easily add up to something tragically less. The truth is, we can struggle unknowingly for our entire lives against what God wants, all the while assuming we are living according to His will.

A grapevine's natural tendency, you see, is *not* abundance. In fact, one expert describes the plant's natural growing tendency as "undisciplined, scattered, and dispersed." Left to itself, a grape plant rambles through the underbrush. It straggles over rocks and climbs up any handy tree trunk. In the process, it manages to produce only small, often bitter fruit.

But in cultivation, the picture changes completely. One grape plant can easily yield sixty large, sweet clusters of grapes each season. One life can, by God's grace, be a trophy for His glory.

Take the life of country preacher John Bunyan. In seventeenth-century England, he spent twelve years of his life in jail for preaching the gospel. When he was offered his freedom on the condition that he stop evangelizing, Bunyan replied, "If I were out of prison today, I would preach the gospel again tomorrow with the help of God."

Bunyan used his prison years to allow God to cultivate his branch. He wrote *Pilgrim's Progress,* a spiritual classic that has been leading thousands to Christ every year since it was published. What Bunyan wanted more than freedom was a life that mattered for God.

Looking back on his imprisonment, Bunyan said, "If I were fruitless, it mattered not who commended me; but if I were fruitful, I cared not who did condemn."

Notice how Bunyan evaluated his success. Were his efforts producing results for eternity? Then he was an unqualified success. His only goal was God's goal for him. That's how you produce spiritual fruit, my friend!

As you look over your life today, to what degree would you say it is entirely given over to accomplishing what God wants? Are you willing to submit to God's hand, to let Him cultivate you—even through adversity—so that you can bear fruit for Him?

If so, then you're on your way to a vigorous and purposeful life, magnificently weighted down with clusters of the most beautiful fruit you've ever seen.

MY VINEYARD JOURNAL: *How much do I truly desire fruitfulness? What can I point to in my life right now that is a sure sign of fruit that brings God glory?*

The one thing He commands us as His branches is to bear fruit.
Live to bless others, to testify of the life and the love there is in Jesus.
In faith and obedience give your whole life to that which Jesus
chose us for and appointed us to—fruit bearing.
Think of His electing us to this, accepting your appointment as coming
from Him Who always gives us everything He demands of us.

ANDREW MURRAY

LET *in the* LIGHT

*For we are His workmanship, created in Christ Jesus for good works,
which God prepared beforehand that we should walk in them.*

EPHESIANS 2:10

O ne day a funny thought came to me: Could I improve an
elephant? I gave it my best shot, but…no luck. For what it
was created to do and where it thrives, the elephant is a work of pure
genius! I tried to come up with improvements for other wonders of
creation—a daffodil, a sunset, a porpoise, a strawberry. Still no luck.
Then reality hit. How could I, one of God's created beings, improve
on something my Creator had already perfected? His creation is
simply miracle upon miracle, repeated over and over again.

And *you* are that kind of miracle too. You are God's intentional,
highly cherished creation. Paul says it beautifully—"We are His
workmanship created in Christ Jesus" (Ephesians 2:10). Not only are
you a masterpiece, you are a masterpiece with a mission—"created in
Christ Jesus for good works" (v. 10).

I wonder if you feel like God's workmanship today, created
specifically for a life of significance and purpose. I hope you do. So
many Christians I know do not. They feel permanently burdened by

regrets, injuries, or shame from past events or current shortcomings. They feel more like a bruised cull or a sorry mess than God's own one-of-a-kind marvel, created in Jesus for good works.

On a recent flight I sat next to Denny, an exceptionally successful businessman and former youth group leader. Later that day he'd be putting ink to a multimillion-dollar contract with NASA. But inside he felt like one big mistake. He told me his third marriage had just collapsed. "I've strayed so far from God and I'm so messed up, I don't know if I can ever come back," he shared with considerable anguish. "Do you think God can ever use me again?"

I told him it was not in his power to destroy what God had created him to do. "And right now, in this airplane," I told Denny, "God is at work in your life to help you reclaim your future."

You, too, may feel bent by past failures, broken by besetting sins, blighted by shame or guilt. But you are still alive in Christ. The sap of eternity still courses through you. When a branch in Christ gets bent or broken, it doesn't die. New growth is waiting to spring forth. Your branch may never look quite the same, but you are still *created in Christ Jesus for good works.* There's no Plan B. God's picture of your future is still a life brimming with extraordinary abundance....

If you choose it.

I'm aware that if you feel more like a mistake than a miracle today, the thought of actually bearing eternal fruit—and lots of it—for God's glory may seem highly improbable. You do not expect a life of abundance, so why prepare for it? My friend, you need to face your thinking for what it is—crippling unbelief. Today it spreads over your life like a black cloud keeping out the sun of God's pleasure and strength.

Of course you and I have sinned. Of course we are deeply flawed. Yet only misdirected pride or an inadequate grasp of God's character and power can separate us from our created purpose. When we respond in humility and repentance, God is ready to pursue that one-of-a-kind purpose in us, starting now.

If I've described your feelings today, I ask you to do something. Let the Lord's truth dispel that black cloud. Let the light of the truth reach your branch today. And then prepare to flourish!

Here are three truths of fruit bearing that you should remind yourself of each day:

- *I am God's workmanship.*
- *I have been created in Christ Jesus for good works.*
- *God's plan for me is a purposeful and abundant life.*

Write these life-changing declarations down. Think about them. Own them. They describe the life God made you for. And He's waiting now to see if you still want it.

MY VINEYARD JOURNAL: *What "black cloud" beliefs about myself do I need to put aside without delay so I can receive the life-giving light of God?*

I thank God for my handicaps,
for through them I have found myself, my work, and my God.

HELEN KELLER

Results Matter

*"By this My Father is glorified, that you bear much fruit;
so you will be My disciples."*

John 15:8

I magine you're in an Italian hilltop village four hundred years ago. It's a bright autumn day, perfect for the annual wine growers' festival. For as long as families here can remember, townspeople have filled the square on Saturday of harvest week for the yearly vinedressers' competition. Honors for the master vinedresser will go to the grower whose best branch can bring in the most grapes.

The crowd cheers as the first contestant enters the square. His pack animal carries a basket piled high with fruit. When he arrives in the square, you watch him lift his basket onto an enormous scale. "Ah! Bellissimo!" people around you exclaim.

As the parade of men and loaded burros continues into the square, the crowd buzzes excitedly. What a year for grapes! Several of the growers need a second basket to haul in their entries. The competition will definitely be close.

When the last grower, white-haired Ernesto, turns the corner into town, the crowd cheers. Then gasps. The burro following him is weighted down with a basket on each side, *each one* overflowing with purple clusters. Spontaneous applause sweeps the square. The man next to you shouts, "How does Ernesto do it?"

But wait! Another burro tethered to the first is rounding the corner. And it carries two more baskets, each brimming with more beautiful grapes!

The crowd erupts. Men, women, and children shout, "Magnifico! Ernesto is the winner! Ernesto will be remembered always!" It seems there'll be no need for a scale this year to know whom to honor as master vinedresser....

Can you guess why I'm telling you this story? In the vineyard that night, Jesus revealed precisely what gives God glory. It is not your intentions. It isn't merely how hard you try. It is how much fruit comes from your branch—"By this my Father is glorified, that you bear *much fruit.*"

I want you to notice the word *much.* Clearly, results matter to God. Each branch bears a different amount of fruit, and all fruit honors God. But God's greatest glory comes from the ones who bear *much* fruit.

Does it surprise you to know that *quantity* matters to God?

We're used to the fact that results count in sports or business. Yet when it comes to our faith, we balk. In fact, in my experience most Christians are likely to say something like, "It's your heart that counts," or "I'm only responsible to try hard."

But consider Jesus' parable about the ten minas in Luke 19:12–27. When the nobleman in Jesus' story returned and called his servants to give an accounting of the money he had entrusted them with, the man who multiplied the master's money the most was rewarded the most. The nobleman's response makes perfect sense in the world of business, but—let me warn you—it rattles most believers to the core.

If you look closely at Jesus' teaching in John 15, you'll notice four levels of fruit bearing:

- Level 1. No fruit ("Every branch in Me that *does not bear fruit,*" v. 2, emphasis added).
- Level 2. Fruit ("every branch that bears *fruit,*" v. 2).
- Level 3. More fruit ("that it may bear *more fruit,*" v. 2).
- Level 4. Much fruit ("bears *much fruit,*" vv. 5, 8).

Where do you think your level of fruit bearing is at this very moment? If the Master Vinedresser harvested your branch this year for His glory, how much honor would He receive? A lot? Some? A little? None?

If you sense that you are among those branches that could bear a lot more fruit, take heart! God cares so much about the outcome of your life that you can count on Him to work continuously in your life toward a harvest of extraordinary abundance and great acclaim for Him.

The secrets of the vineyard that you'll learn in the weeks to come will show you how the Master Vinedresser is at work to move you from one level up to the next and then the next. Once you accept the responsibility of cooperating with Him to bear a lot of fruit for God, you'll begin to see the beautiful results of a life that is destined to add luster to His name for eternity.

MY VINEYARD JOURNAL: *How do I feel about my current level of fruit bearing? What do I see in my life that leads me to conclude I'm producing at this level?*

*It is God who works in you
both to will and to do for His good pleasure.*

PHILIPPIANS 2:13

VISIBLE PROOF

Beloved, I beg you as sojourners and pilgrims, abstain from fleshly lusts which war against the soul, having your conduct honorable among the Gentiles, that when they speak against you as evildoers, they may, by your good works which they observe, glorify God in the day of visitation.

1 PETER 2:11–12

Most greatly used men and women in God's kingdom can point to a day in their life when they made a formal decision to live for God's glory.

One Sunday afternoon in 1951, in a little bungalow in Los Angeles, a young married couple signed their names to a "transfer of ownership." Their dreams, their possessions and passions, their abilities and liabilities, their years—all were signed over to God by the stroke of a pen. No one witnessed the signing. And Bill and Vonette Bright had no idea what would come next. But God did.

Fifty years later, the student outreach they started—Campus Crusade for Christ—has grown into sixty separate ministries worldwide, touching almost every segment of society. A pamphlet Dr. Bright wrote, called *Have You Heard of the Four Spiritual Laws?* has been used over three billion times. Campus Crusade's evangelistic film, *Jesus,* has been viewed by 4 billion people in 233 countries, resulting in more than 121 million people coming to salvation.

One stroke of the pen...

How much of the ownership of your life have you consciously given over to bringing God credit in this world? The very fact that you're reading this book means that you sincerely desire to serve God in a significant way. Yet our words and actions don't serve God unless our purposes belong to Him as well. For example, we can mistake feeling fulfilled and significant in Christian service as proof that we're glorifying God.

So how can we know we're bringing God public glory, not just living a pretty good life? Here's a simple way to think about it:

God is glorified when an onlooker—particularly an unbeliever— observes you sacrificially doing something good for a recipient and is compelled to say, "Thank God for what that person did! Who is the wonderful God behind this?"

Jesus put it this way: "Let your light so shine before men, that they may see your good works and glorify your Father in heaven" (Matthew 5:16).

I wonder today if you or your church has ever intentionally set out to meet specific, unmet needs with only two requirements: 1) You get nothing in return (maybe not even a "warm fuzzy"); and 2) God's reputation receives a huge boost. It strikes me that if you went around the neighborhoods of most churches and asked, "Have you ever thanked God for that church up the street?" you'd come away shocked at how many would say no.

A couple of days ago I spoke to Dr. Bright on the phone. Now in declining health and on oxygen support, he's *still* focusing his energies on touching the world for God.

I remember the day in my life when I decided to live for fruit that glorifies God. What a breakthrough that was for me! I urge you to formalize your own decision today. If you've made one in the past, affirm it again before you go on. Nothing you learn in this book will help you unless you have given yourself away to God and to the wonderful pursuit of *His* glory.

Join me, then, in this important declaration:

> *O God, I want only what You want for my life. From this day*
> *forward, I will measure success, achievement, and fulfillment*
> *by doing good works that bring You glory. Today I sign over*
> *ownership of my life to You, asking only that You will use me to*
> *show the world what a wonderful God You are!*

My Vineyard Journal: *Write your prayer in your journal; then sign and date it. Place a copy of your prayer in a prominent place. Carry a copy with you.*

> *The Christian should resemble a fruit tree, not a Christmas tree.*
> *For the gaudy decorations of a Christmas tree are only tied on,*
> *whereas fruit grows on a fruit tree.*
>
> JOHN STOTT

A Trophy Life

"Eye has not seen, nor ear heard,
Nor have entered into the heart of man
The things which God has prepared for those who love Him."

1 Corinthians 2:9

It was one for the national record book, a believe-it-or-not whopper that had been told and retold for a thousand years. Every Jewish child had grown up hearing the story of how Moses commissioned twelve of his champion warriors to scout the Promised Land. And how, when they returned to camp, they brought back a most amazing trophy....

One cluster of grapes so huge it took two men just to carry it!

Think I'm exaggerating? The Bible says, "They came to the Valley of Eshcol, and there cut down a branch with one cluster of grapes; they carried it between two of them on a pole" (Numbers 13:23). For Israel, that one enormous cluster stood as proof that God's best for His children would always be shockingly greater than anything they could imagine for themselves.

God's work in our lives can produce a harvest like that, too—remarkable, unheard-of, obviously supernatural in origin, memorable for generations.

Now that you know what real fruit looks like (something you do that brings God glory) and that results matter, you're ready to discover, perhaps for the first time, your own level of fruitfulness. Yesterday I asked you how much glory your branch is bringing God. Let me ask you now, if the Vinedresser came by your branch today, collected all the clusters of grapes, and put them in His basket, how full would it be?

Give the question some thought, then check the statement that best shows what you think God would see as the current level of fruitfulness in your life:

_____ Level 1. God would see *no fruit* in my basket.

_____ Level 2. God would see *some fruit* in my basket.

_____ Level 3. God would see *quite a bit of fruit* in my basket.

_____ Level 4. God would see *a lot of fruit* in my basket.

How do you feel about your answer? Encouraged? Frustrated? Embarrassed?

Take the time you need today to write out in your journal your answers to some important questions:

- Why did you place yourself where you did? Describe the circumstances in your life that lead you to believe you are bearing fruit—or not.
- What are several ways you can see yourself bearing new fruit in the future? Based on your gifts and talents, what kinds of good

works or acts of ministry do you long for or sense that God might lead you to do?

• How motivated are you to move to the next level of fruitfulness, and what do you believe it will take to get there? Are you willing?

I hope that this week's readings have stirred in you an increasing desire for extraordinary fruitfulness for God. In weeks to come, we're going to explore together how God comes alongside of your life to help you take the next step toward greater productivity and fulfillment.

Remember, what God has in mind for you is so far beyond what you are experiencing right now that you can't possibly imagine it. You—one magnificent branch in the Father's vineyard—were made for abundance, God desires it, and He is actively at work in your life right now to bring it about.

Because what He sees when He sees you is a trophy life for Him.

My Vineyard Journal: *"Lord, change me with the truth, even the truth I don't want to face. Use my answers to today's questions to move me toward a life that honors You and brings You pleasure."*

He who sows to his flesh will of the flesh reap corruption,
but he who sows to the Spirit will of the Spirit reap everlasting life.
And let us not grow weary while doing good,
for in due season we shall reap if we do not lose heart.

Galatians 6:8–9

Let me offer You in sacrifice the service
of my thoughts and my tongue,
but first give me what I may offer You.

Augustine of Hippo

Week Two

LIFTED UP
by LOVE

Direct my steps by Your word,
And let no iniquity have dominion over me.

PSALM 119:133

FROM BARREN *to* BOUNTIFUL

My son, do not despise the chastening of the LORD,
Nor detest His correction;
For whom the LORD loves He corrects,
Just as a father the son in whom he delights.

PROVERBS 3:11–12

Rosie, a high-energy professional, was telling me about her first "career" as a teenage berry picker. "We used to get up at the crack of dawn to catch the farm bus out to the fields. We worked long hours for not a lot of money. By the time we fell into bed at night we never wanted to see another berry. 'Course, then we dreamed about nothing but berries all night long!"

"So how long did your career in berries last?" I asked.

"Oh, about a week," she said. I expressed surprise. Turns out Rosie hit a career snag named Vince. "He was so cute," she told me, laughing. "And I was young. I spent more time chasing him than picking berries. One afternoon, my row boss noticed my bucket was empty again. That was it. She said, 'Rosie, honey, why don't you sleep in tomorrow. Your berry season is over.'"

Plenty of adults I know can identify with Rosie's unpromising start in the working world. Unfortunately, too many Christians can also identify with a spiritual basket which keeps coming up empty.

Jesus told His disciples, "Every branch in Me that does not bear fruit He takes away" (John 15:2). Notice that fruit bearing is optional. Unlike a grape plant, a believer can decide not to bear fruit. Let me ask you—have you gone a day, a week, or even months when you chose to live in such a way that your life produced no fruit for God? Christian audiences around the world overwhelmingly identify with that question, agreeing that barren periods have occurred in their spiritual lives.

But what does the Vinedresser do when a branch in His vineyard chooses to remain barren? Fruitlessness certainly isn't His will for us. Does "takes away" in this verse mean that, like an impatient row boss, God gives up on you and puts you in the discard pile?

My personal understanding of this question came unexpectedly. One day I met a second-generation vineyard owner from California, and I asked him why some branches don't bear fruit. He explained that some branches fall from the trellis and trail along the ground. They get covered with dust and mud and soon become diseased.

"What do you do then?" I asked. "Cut them off?"

"Oh no!" he exclaimed. "Branches are much too valuable for that. We go through the rows looking for them. We carefully lift them up, wash them off, and tie them back to the trellis. Pretty soon they're thriving again."

His comments drove me to reexamine the Bible text, and what I found there made sense for the first time. You see, a better translation of the Greek verb *airo*—here rendered "take away"—is "take up" or "lift up." *Airo* is the same word Jesus used when He told the lame man, *"Take up* your bed, and go to your house" (Matthew 9:6).

Do you see the picture now too? For the Christian, sin is like dirt covering your leaves. It makes your branch sick and keeps you from bearing fruit. God grieves when your branch is barren, not only because He's seeing no fruit but also because you're not thriving. But He won't throw you away. Instead, He kneels by your branch, gently cleanses you, then lifts you back up to a productive, God-honoring life.

This is the first secret of the vine: *When we choose to languish in sin, God intervenes to motivate us to stop sinning and begin bearing fruit again.*

The Bible describes this process as discipline or chastening. But you and I could call it "love lifting me."

MY VINEYARD JOURNAL: *How does the idea that God might be disciplining me make me feel?*

&

> *He who keeps instruction is in the way of life,*
> *But he who refuses correction goes astray.*
>
> PROVERBS 10:17

> *Man still wishes to be happy even when*
> *he so lives as to make happiness impossible.*
>
> AUGUSTINE OF HIPPO

Johnny *in* Sleepers

This is what the LORD says—your Redeemer, the Holy One of Israel:
"I am the LORD your God, who teaches you what is best for you,
who directs you in the way you should go. If only you had paid
attention to my commands, your peace would have been like a river,
your righteousness like the waves of the sea."

ISAIAH 48:17–18, NIV

Mom and Dad have tucked Johnny in for the night and curled up on the couch for TV and some quiet conversation…and then Johnny pads into the room tugging on his sleepers. After Dad makes sure his little boy doesn't need or want anything—except *not* to stay in bed—Johnny gets sent back to bed with a reprimand. Mom and Dad settle back.

Five minutes later, Johnny is standing in the doorway again, thumb in mouth.

This time Johnny gets a swat. In fact, over the next forty-five minutes Johnny gets quite a few swats as the scenario repeats itself over and over. *Why can't Johnny get it through his head,* the exasperated parents wonder, *that if he gets out of bed he'll experience unhappy consequences?*

Obviously, Johnny believes something that isn't true. But what?

That the swats are not connected to his behavior? That next time his parents won't notice? That a specific bedtime for kids is a bad idea?

I've noticed that we Christians can be a lot like Johnny in sleepers. We keep padding into trouble because we can't see—or refuse to see—any connection between our short-sighted behaviors and any distress we might be experiencing.

To show you what I mean, I've asked audiences all over the world to give me their frank assessment on three closely linked issues. Here's what they've told me:

- When I've asked, "What percentage of Christians do you believe are in each of the four levels of fruit bearing?" audiences have repeatedly estimated that at any given time up to 65 percent of believers are bearing no fruit for God—not even one grape.

- The same audiences estimate that most Christians do not believe that God actively disciplines His children when they stray. Putting that observation in vineyard terms, most Christians assume the Vinedresser does nothing when He sees that their branch is withering and unfruitful.

- Which leads naturally to their final observation: Three-fourths of all Christians don't make any connection between unaddressed sin in their lives and personal distress or painful circumstances they may be experiencing.

These statements are truly sobering. Since we know that God wants a huge harvest, but we observe that the majority of His branches are not producing fruit, we must conclude that God's intervening discipline is widespread and intensifying.

Meet Paul, a university student. He told me, "Honestly, Bruce, I don't think God is dealing with me now because I'm still sinning a lot." Later, Paul admitted that his life was in a downward spiral and that he frequently prayed that God would fix his negative circumstances and feelings. But he is behaving like Johnny in sleepers. He is making no connection between his increasingly stressful experience and God's response to his sin. And rather than change his behavior, Paul keeps asking God to stop what He is doing to address the problem. As you'd guess, Paul's prayers don't seem to get results.

Do you recognize yourself in these statements? Have you been misinterpreting unwanted circumstances and emotions as random events when they are actually God's discipline in your life?

If so, get ready for quite an awakening. In the days ahead, you'll learn more about how you can cooperate with God to step out of discipline and into a new season of spiritual plenty. It will be one of the best moves you ever make. A friend told me about his experience in discipline: "I know God wasn't pleased with my choices back then, but you know, I wasn't pleased with them either. I didn't have peace. My life just didn't count for much. What in the world was I thinking!"

MY VINEYARD JOURNAL: *"Lord, please reveal to me any wrong beliefs, behaviors, or attitudes that are blinding me to what You're trying to do in my life. I want to know—and live—the truth."*

Discipline puts back in its place that something in us which should serve but wants to rule.

ANONYMOUS

DEGREES *of* INTERVENTION

You have forgotten the exhortation which speaks to you as to sons:
"My son, do not despise the chastening of the LORD,
Nor be discouraged when you are rebuked by Him;
For whom the LORD loves He chastens,
And scourges every son whom He receives."

HEBREWS 12:5–6

For many of us, the idea that God actively disciplines us comes as an uncomfortable surprise. *Why would God want to cause me pain?* we wonder. *I thought He loved me!* That's why understanding the hows and whys of discipline is critical if we're going to flourish in God's vineyard.

In our passage in Hebrews today, we find several key principles:

God's discipline is personal, applied with just the individual branch in mind. If you're a parent, you know that what motivates one child may not even get another's attention. The Vinedresser works in your life in the same way.

God's discipline is purposeful, steering us away from sin and toward abundance.

God's discipline is progressive, starting with the least pressure necessary. In today's passage, three levels or degrees of intervention are set forth. God begins with:

- Degree 1—*rebuke* (v. 5). Like any loving father, God doesn't enjoy causing us pain of any kind. That's why His Spirit first prompts you: "You really should stop that now. You know I'm not pleased with what you're doing." We hear God's rebuke in a word of Scripture, through another person, by a prick of the conscience, or by the direct conviction of the Holy Spirit.

But if we don't respond, He moves from rebuke to:

- Degree 2—*chastening* (v. 6). Here we experience emotional turmoil and increasing pressure, both internally and externally. Circumstances seem set against us. Our spiritual life seems permanently in the doldrums. God is using increasing discomfort to get us to stop our harmful behavior.

However, if we persist in rebelling, the intensity of discipline increases again:

- Degree 3—*scourging* (v. 6). Scourging is severe pain or trauma intended to make further straying more and more unbearable. *Scourge* is the same word the Gospels use to describe how the Romans whipped Jesus before His execution (John 19:1). It might have shocked you to read that "every son whom He receives" experiences scourging. That means if you know Jesus Christ as your personal Savior, you have undoubtedly been scourged.

At this level of rebellion, you are probably living in open sin and willfully disregarding what you know God wants. You haven't responded to rebuke or chastening. Therefore, God resorts to severe pain to get your attention. In 1 Corinthians 11:17–32, Paul reports on the misery, illness, and even death (v. 30) that has come to a church body because of continual, serious, willful sin among its members. Clearly, the Father takes long-term sin very seriously, and He *will* act.

My friend, I know that *rebuke, chasten,* and *scourge* are not likable words. They don't sell books or attract newcomers to church. Yet discipline in God's family is full of promise and hope. In fact, every word is couched in relationship: "You have forgotten the exhortation that speaks to you as *sons...*"(12:5) says the writer of Hebrews. And "...*whom the Lord loves* He chastens" (v. 6).

If you're tangled up in serious sin today, your Father's first desire is that you stop it. That's where the life you really want starts. All day long, Your Father will be speaking to you as a son or daughter. And He won't give up, even when He hurts.

MY VINEYARD JOURNAL: *Can I look back and see a time when God was disciplining me on one of these levels (rebuke, chastening, scourging)? Did I recognize it as God's discipline then?*

Harsh discipline is for him who forsakes the way,
And he who hates correction will die.

PROVERBS 15:10

THE PERFECT DISCIPLINARIAN

We have had human fathers who corrected us, and we paid them respect.
Shall we not much more readily be in subjection to the Father of spirits
and live? For they indeed for a few days chastened us as seemed best to
them, but He for our profit, that we may be partakers of His holiness.
Now no chastening seems to be joyful for the present, but painful;
nevertheless, afterward it yields the peaceable fruit of righteousness
to those who have been trained by it.

HEBREWS 12:9–11

Chandra, a doctoral student from India, told me she nearly always chokes on the second word of the Lord's Prayer. She loves Jesus, but thinking of God as Father? That's difficult. Her own father molested her from the time she was four until she ran away at fifteen.

So many today have grown up in destructive homes. I think of Will, whose father took physical punishment to such extremes that Will still walks with a limp. And Helen, who grew up in a home where parental discipline vanished the day her father walked out, never to return.

There's something about discipline that brings us right to the big questions about God the Father: What is His nature? What are His motives? What is His record? Can He be trusted with our hearts and lives?

The writer of Hebrews understood that although earthly fathers aren't perfect, God is. If we listen to our flawed earthly fathers, he argued, why don't we give the utmost respect and heed to our perfect heavenly Father?

Today I want you to open your heart to a life-changing truth: God is the perfect disciplinarian. Every time He intervenes to free you from a destructive choice, His action is lovingly and wisely custom-suited to your need. For example:

- *His methods are perfect.* God never abuses or heedlessly injures His children. He's never too harsh or too lenient. God has unlimited options. He uses people, circumstances, and events—and if we resist one, He can and will raise up another.
- *His motives are perfect.* Our Father doesn't lose His temper. He doesn't release His rage on a straying child. He doesn't exact payment or even the score. He is never unkind and receives no personal satisfaction when He disciplines us.
- *His commitment is perfect.* God will proactively pursue us until we start cleaning up our act. He values our obedience more than our comfort—or His. He will discipline us even if we don't believe He will, even if we turn our backs on Him.

Of course, not all inconvenience, frustration, doubt, and suffering are God-induced. We live in a fallen world where evil people, disease, and natural disasters can strike at any time. Yet the Bible makes it clear that God will even use suffering to get our attention.

Do you see it? Your heavenly Father is compelled by love to intervene in your life when you insist on behaviors that sabotage your present and your future.

Does it feel good to you? Not at all.

Does your Father *want* to cause you discomfort or anguish? Of course not.

Will your Father stop pursuing you with His best? Not even when you break His heart!

As you go about your day, let these wonderful truths of your Father's love remain in your thoughts:

- *My Father loves me.*
- *My Father is patiently seeking my best.*
- *My Father will never give up on me.*

Ask your Father to take these words about His nature and intentions deep into your memories, thoughts, and emotions. And ask Him to change you with the truth.

MY VINEYARD JOURNAL: *When I think of God as my Father, what feelings am I most likely to experience? Will these feelings help or hinder when He disciplines me?*

🍇

Now may our Lord Jesus Christ Himself, and our God and Father, who has loved us and given us everlasting consolation and good hope by grace, comfort your hearts and establish you in every good word and work.

2 THESSALONIANS 2:16–17

OLD BUSINESS

Create in me a clean heart, O God,
And renew a steadfast spirit within me.

PSALM 51:10

Scientists say that most chemical waste on our planet ends up being dumped into holes in the ground. Once these poisons seep into the soil and taint water supplies, serious damage can result. And the toxic threat can last for decades, even centuries.

All of us carry trash from the past into our lives in Christ. By trash I mean destructive behaviors, hurtful attitudes, or unresolved conflicts. Often we try to keep these sins buried like toxic waste, hoping we can keep them deep enough that they won't affect us, hoping no one will notice, hoping above all that they will eventually disappear.

But they don't. Over time, they affect other areas of our lives, often in surprising ways. We flounder in relationships. We can't seem to get anything out of church. We lose interest in Bible reading. Our spiritual development seems sidelined. Perhaps our health suffers. Real fruitfulness for God seems permanently out of reach, and we don't know why.

I remember sitting on a hillside in Southern Oregon when I was in my late twenties. The early morning sun slanted across neatly tended pear orchards. It was a beautiful spot—but I was in desperate days with the Lord. For some time I had felt that I couldn't break through invisible barriers in my personal life and ministry. That morning I prayed, *Lord, if there is anything in my past that hinders our relationship, let me know now.*

Then I took out a yellow legal pad and began writing down the things that came to mind. Three pages later I was still writing. It was the longest list of unfinished personal business I'd ever seen.

Have you been in such a place? If so, then you know that a mountain of reluctance, rationalization, and fear rose up to keep me from actually doing something about it.

But with God's help I followed through. I made phone calls. I made confessions and asked for forgiveness. I acted on old, forgotten commitments. In time every piece of "trash" was disposed of. And I began to experience a deeply settled confidence, a cleanness of heart, and a revitalized emotional and spiritual life.

My friend Chuck Colson has said, "One of the great myths of Christianity is that once a person is converted, they never sin again. On the contrary, we're fighting a constant battle. It's like we're running up a hill that's well-greased—you make it a couple of steps forward and then you slide back."

Every day the Vinedresser is ready to help us cleanse ourselves of musty old sins that are polluting our spirit and preventing genuine abundance.

Why wait?

If you're ready to respond, the Holy Spirit is ready to lend supernatural strength to your decision (see Philippians 2:13). With a writing pad in hand, ask God to show you what old, unfinished business is stopping you from bearing fruit for Him. Write it all down. Then confess each sin to Him one at a time. Begin immediately to ask forgiveness of others, make restitution, or mend relationships as needed.

When we respond to God's conviction in a specific area, something extraordinary happens: Discipline ends *immediately*. Our Father, who has been watching and waiting for this moment, runs toward us with outstretched arms, His best robe in hand and a family celebration in mind. (Watch how the Father responded to a son's return in the parable of the Prodigal Son, Luke 15:11–32.)

I promise you'll wonder what it was about that stinky old trash that was worth keeping you away from your Father's delight and a new start on life.

My Vineyard Journal: *"Lord, show me what sins are blocking me from bearing fruit for You. Help me to make things right...."*

When you have a right-standing relationship with God,
you have a life of freedom, liberty, and delight;
you are God's will.

Oswald Chambers

"You-Turn"

For godly sorrow produces repentance leading to salvation,
not to be regretted; but the sorrow of the world produces death.

2 Corinthians 7:10

Think of God's discipline as traffic signs along the road of your life. Some quietly caution. Some sternly direct. Some nearly shout alarm.

Yet every message of discipline, whether gentle or urgent, provides vital information. In spiritual terms, these messages are intended to lead us to repentance—a change of mind and direction, away from sin and toward God. For believers, it's the most important "you-turn" we'll ever take.

In Day 10 of this week, we talked about the different degrees of God's intervention. Today I want you to meet two outstanding Bible leaders who responded very differently to the road signs. Each was a man who had been fruitful for God and came to a "you-turn" in his life. In that moment, one chose to ignore the signs and paid a great price; the other turned and received a great victory.

LEADER ONE: A GOOD MAN SAYS NO TO GOD'S DISCIPLINE.

King Asa, great-great-grandson of David, grew up to love God and serve Him despite being raised by parents who did not. Asa was a good king who initiated many reforms. In his later years, however, he started to trust his allies more than God. When a prophet confronted him, King Asa angrily threw the man in prison.

From that moment, Asa's benevolent rule turned sour, and he began to suffer severe health problems (see 2 Chronicles 16:10–13).

Don't miss the stages of Asa's slide toward disaster: He didn't listen to rebuke; then, instead of responding to God's chastening, he vented it on others (v. 10); finally, he even refused to repent under scourging. The Bible says, "His malady was severe; yet in his disease he did not seek the LORD" (v. 12). And Asa died in great agony.

What a tragic end to a once-promising life!

LEADER TWO: A GOOD MAN SAYS YES TO GOD'S DISCIPLINE.

King Josiah, a descendant of David, grew up to love and serve God despite being the son and grandson of kings who did not. He was a good king who initiated many reforms (starting to sound familiar?). While remodeling the temple his workers discovered "the Book of the Law in the house of the LORD" (2 Kings 22:8). Josiah immediately asked a scribe to read it to him.

Convicted by how far the nation had strayed from God's Word, the king wept, repented, and tore his robe. He called national leaders together to hear the Scriptures; then he made a public pledge to follow the Lord fully.

The result? Through a prophet, God told Josiah, "Because your heart was tender, and you humbled yourself before the LORD when you heard what I spoke…I also have heard you" (2 Kings 22:19). It was the beginning of a major nationwide revival. In fact, Josiah's reign became a high point in Israel's history.

For Josiah, a quick response to the first sign of trouble ended God's intervention and invited enormous blessings.

Take a minute to evaluate what signs God might be putting in your path today. For a review of how to recognize the different degrees of discipline, refer back to Day 10.

If God is rebuking you, I urge you to listen to what you know is right and do it. You will lose more than you gain by waiting.

If you're in chastening, you have already resisted God too long and paid too great a price. The stress and opposition you feel today are God's urgent call to you: "Get out of this sin before its consequences become even more severe."

If you're in scourging, let me ask you, How hard is your heart over this ongoing, serious sin? Have you gotten used to saying, "I'm just made this way," or "I think God has given up on me"? If so, watch out! Great trauma and regret may lie ahead. I beg you to turn around.

Repentance is a "you-turn" toward God's will. It's something only we can choose to do. And it's always the first move toward the abundant life for any of God's wayward daughters and sons.

MY VINEYARD JOURNAL: *Can I recall a time when my sin brought me to tears? How did I feel after I repented? What could possibly be keeping me from repenting of sin right now?*

"I have blotted out, like a thick cloud, your transgressions,
And like a cloud, your sins.
Return to Me, for I have redeemed you."

ISAIAH 44:22

Bear fruits worthy of repentance.

LUKE 3:8

GOD'S SURPRISE MOVES

When the morning had now come, Jesus stood on the shore;
yet the disciples did not know that it was Jesus. Then Jesus said to them,
"Children, have you any food?" They answered Him, "No."
And He said to them, "Cast the net on the right side of the boat,
and you will find some." So they cast, and now they were not
able to draw it in because of the multitude of fish.

JOHN 21:4–6

You've spent a week looking more deeply into the process of "lifting up"—the acts of God in our lives that are specifically intended to separate us from the sins that put a blight on our relationships and our productivity. The very fact that you have had the courage to face this serious discussion each day says something important about you: You hunger after God, and you won't let your sins—even the ones you struggle with the most—keep you very long from seeking His best for your life.

It's important that you know that, because it's true. You have a promising future in your Father's vineyard. Peter shared this same determination to follow Jesus, even after he had failed Him badly....

And he proved it with one bold leap.

You remember the scene from John 21:1–19. Peter and several other disciples had returned to fishing after the Crucifixion. It was early morning on the lake. Shorebirds piped in the reeds, boats bumped and creaked in the mist, and water dripped from the nets as the men worked. But there was no sign of fish.

Peter's nets were empty spiritually as well as physically. He was still "in Christ," but sin was preventing any kind of harvest. He had stopped fishing for men and returned to fishing for fish. In vineyard terms, his branch was blighted and barren. And we know why—only days before, he had caved in to fear and denied his Lord.

Pause today to consider how Jesus responded to Peter. You'd think such grievous sin would warrant more intense discipline. But after the men finally landed their nets full of fish, Jesus invited them to sit down for breakfast. And after breakfast, He offered Peter the gentlest of rebukes. Simply a question—"Do you love Me?" (vv. 15–17).

To me, this scene is a poignant reminder of two of God's mercy-filled, surprise moves in our own lives. For example:

- *God does not discipline for every sin.* A parent acts when he sees a pattern developing or a wrong attitude taking root; he doesn't impose discipline on a child for every misbehavior. In the same way, God is not poised over our lives, ready to strike at the first sign of sin.

- *God may not discipline us immediately after we sin, giving us time to repent on our own.* You might even pray, "Be merciful to me. Please give me time to repent."

These "mercy surprises" that God extends to us always have a wonderful purpose. The Bible says that God is "longsuffering toward us…that all should come to repentance" (2 Peter 3:9).

Commenting on Peter's restoration, the late Roy Hicks Jr. wrote in *A Small Book About God:* "What breaks your heart and mine is being forced to recognize that even though we have failed Him miserably, we genuinely do love Him. We have failed Him—only to discover that He doesn't want to talk about our failures. He wants to talk about our love."

How shocking it is to come out of a season of discipline knowing that God is more kind and giving than you ever dared hope and that you want to do His will more than you ever thought possible.

As we close this week together, take several minutes for a conversation with your Father. Look back over your past rebellions. Apologize for hurtful choices. Thank Him for His steadfast kindness and unflinching commitment to your welfare. Tell Him you serve Him for His pleasure—and yours.

And look forward to more of God's surprises in pruning, your next season in His vineyard.

MY VINEYARD JOURNAL: *Do I respond to sin by repenting or by running from Jesus? How might experiencing God's mercy and letting it penetrate my heart change the way I respond when I've sinned?*

The fear of the Lord is the beginning of knowledge.
But fools despise wisdom and instruction.

PROVERBS 1:7

Week Three

REACHING

for the BEST

*God's fingers can touch nothing
but to mould it into loveliness.*

GEORGE MACDONALD

MAKING ROOM *for* MORE

"My Father is the vinedresser.... Every branch that bears fruit
He prunes, that it may bear more fruit."

JOHN 15:1–2

The day before I bought your book *Secrets of the Vine*, I happened to be in my backyard staring at a grapevine," the letter reads. It's from a California woman named Hazel. "I've been watering that silly vine for ten years, always wondering why we've never gotten any edible grapes off of it even though it's lush and beautiful. But we have never pruned it. God has a wonderful sense of timing, don't you think?"

Do you identify with Hazel's bemused realization? I do. How easy it is to mistake doing a good thing for doing the best thing, or living a full life for cultivating a fruitful one.

This week we will discover how our generous God leads us toward genuine spiritual bounty now that more fruit production, and not less sin, is the main issue. Jesus called this process pruning.

Every gardener knows that pruning means cutting. One guide defines pruning as "removing unwanted plant parts for a purpose." The gardener removes unnecessary branches and useless offshoots.

He pinches back buds to redirect growth. He thins excessive fruit to get bigger fruit.

The result? The plant flourishes for its intended purpose.

In our spiritual lives, pruning is an ongoing, intimate interaction with a pleased and hopeful Vinedresser. In pruning we sense a recurring invitation. God is calling us away from less important occupations to our full potential and significance. He comes repeatedly to tend our branch so that even though we are doing some things well, we will be able to do more things outstandingly. That's why we can say yes to Him with great anticipation!

I call this truth the second secret of the vine: *If your life bears some fruit, God will repeatedly intervene to prune you so that you will bear even more fruit.*

Since every branch in Christ gets pruned, we know that the Vinedresser is at work everywhere in the family of God. Here are some common focal points of God's pruning shears:

- Priorities that need to be rearranged.
- Attachments that weigh us down.
- Values that were acceptable when we were younger but aren't now.
- Busyness that may accomplish much but not what matters most.
- Relationships that diminish our impact instead of enlarging it.

My friend, in all our discussion this week about what God may be trying to remove from your life, remember the surprising truth about pruning: *What feels like loss is really about gain.*

In fact, at times you may feel that what God is asking of you contradicts His character or His promises. But the opposite is true.

He is simply hard at work guiding you toward the life of impact and significance that you've asked for and that He wants to give you.

Pruning is God's way of making room in your life for *more* of what matters most. As you cooperate with Him, you find yourself shaking your head—not over what you have left behind, but at the wonderful results you see flourishing all around.

MY VINEYARD JOURNAL: *What "more" might God be trying to give me today? What "more" do I want most from Him?*

Our heavenly Father never takes anything from His children unless He means to give them something better.
GEORGE MÜLLER

*Therefore we also pray always for you that our God would...
fulfill all the good pleasure of His goodness
and the work of faith with power,
that the name of our Lord Jesus Christ
may be glorified in you, and you in Him,
according to the grace of our God and the Lord Jesus Christ.*

2 THESSALONIANS 1:11–12

CONFESSIONS *of a* LEAF LOVER

Turn away my eyes from looking at worthless things,
And revive me in Your way.
Establish Your word to Your servant,
Who is devoted to fearing You.

PSALM 119:37–38

Y ears ago our family owned an old farm. When we bought the property, I set about "bush hoggin'"—a local term for clearing underbrush with a tractor. In the process I came upon a tangle of grapevines on broken-down trellises. The abandoned plants had nearly smothered the surrounding undergrowth with leafy branches, but the fruit—what I could find of it—was tiny and sour.

When I mentioned the vines to a neighbor, he said, "Oh, you'd never guess by looking at it now, but that used to be a premium vineyard. But the previous owner let it go for years."

John 15 makes it very clear that our Father the Vinedresser loves His chosen ones too much to ever let us go to waste. He is constantly at work in His vineyard, helping us produce a bigger crop and fewer leaves.

Think of "leaves" as those things in our lives, often even good things, that deplete energies, time, and talents. God is trying to get more "sap" to those areas that produce fruit by cutting away what isn't necessary. That involves surrender and relinquishment on our part. And that's where discomfort can come in. We're reluctant to lay something down that feels important to our happiness.

One day before I taught a small group on this subject, I wrote in the margin of my notes, "I've discovered that I'm more a lover of leaves than a farmer of fruit."

That was my confession. It was true, yet thankfully not the complete truth. Here's what I mean. It's easy for me to mistake activities for results, busyness for meaningful pursuits, rampant foliage for an overflowing harvest. The truth is that most of us hardly realize we're leaf lovers until we become fruit lovers! After all, leaves and new shoots are part of flourishing. Yet once you and I start bearing fruit for God, we understand the vineyard better. We realize that less unnecessary foliage means more sap going to fruit. And *more fruit* is the real prize!

Perhaps you can make a similar confession today. The appeal of leaves never quite seems to go away, does it? Yet we know we were born for more.

We may shrink from the pruning shears, but we have been redeemed and chosen for a life of strategic impact and significance for God. In this amazing passage, Jesus shows us that we are being cultivated every day so that we will take a harvest of lasting value into His presence in eternity.

Listen to Jesus' exciting destiny for you and me: "I chose you and appointed you that you should go and bear fruit, and that your fruit should remain" (John 15:16).

When He said to Peter, James, and John, "Leave your nets," He was inviting them to leave one kind of harvest so they could prepare for another, immeasurably better harvest. Why? They weren't chosen to be leaf growers. And they'd never be able to capture their real destiny in a mere net.

They were chosen and appointed for fruit that remains. And so are you.

MY VINEYARD JOURNAL: *"Lord, show me what areas of my life are producing mostly leaves instead of fruit. Show me the things that are crowding out Your best. And lead me toward true fruitfulness today."*

If you love earthly things, you wander far from God—
the body wanders in places; the soul wanders in affections.
To love God is to throw off every spiritual weight
that will keep your soul from rising to Him.

AUGUSTINE OF HIPPO

For our light affliction,
which is but for a moment,
is working for us a far more exceeding
and eternal weight of glory.

2 CORINTHIANS 4:17

SHEAR PANIC

The works of his hands are faithful and just;
all his precepts are trustworthy.

PSALM 111:7, NIV

I t's one thing to imagine God as a loving protector, holding out His strong arms to care for you. But it's quite another to think about the all-powerful God as a vinedresser, coming straight toward you with a pruning instrument.

What if He gets carried away and I end up mangled instead of fruitful? you might wonder.

I'm reminded of a story told by an expert gardener: "One day a friend invited me into his backyard to point out a badly mutilated European highbush cranberry. 'I read somewhere that all shrubs should be pruned occasionally, but I really didn't know how,' he apologized. His intentions were good, but for that poor cranberry bush his lack of knowledge was dangerous."

After looking over the damage, the gardener decided that the cranberry bush would probably survive but that the cuts would have killed a less sturdy plant.

What a scary picture! No wonder when God asks you to let go

of another hindrance in your life, your first reaction can be reluctance or even panic.

What we believe about God is just as critical in pruning as in discipline. I would take that statement further. Your ability to endure pruning and your response to what the Vinedresser is trying to accomplish is completely dependent on how much you trust Him. Every branch needs to know:

- Does the Vinedresser care specifically about my branch?
- Does the Vinedresser prune my branch for my good?
- Will the Vinedresser always prune at the right time in my life?
- Does the Vinedresser use the best method to prune me?
- Does the Vinedresser prune only for as long as necessary?
- Will the Vinedresser stay with me through the process?

When you address these questions honestly, you will sense a door suddenly, silently swinging open in your heart. You will step across a threshold into a place of relinquishment and peace…and you will never want to go back.

Great faith, which releases amazing works of God, always begins with a few rock-solid facts: God is in control. God is good. And God will never stop working for our good, even when we don't recognize what He's doing.

Corrie ten Boom, a prisoner of the Nazis who lost most of her family in the death camps, described in *The Hiding Place* how she rested in God's trustworthiness: "When a train goes through a tunnel and it gets dark, you don't throw away the ticket and jump off. You sit still and trust the engineer."

That expert gardener I mentioned at the beginning of the chapter went on to note: "The basic premise of pruning should be to always have a good reason for making each cut. Pick up the clippers only to correct a faulty growing condition, to prevent a future problem, or to stimulate or redirect new growth."

Are you fearful or resistant about something God is trying to change in your life today? Your all-wise, all-loving, all-powerful Father is at work. With you specifically in mind, He has considered all the options, determined the most important area to focus on, and chosen the perfect time and method.

Today's verse sums up the case for trust—"The works of his hands are faithful and just." That's terrific news for every branch!

MY VINEYARD JOURNAL: *"Lord, show me what aspect of pruning is causing me to doubt Your intentions. Forgive me, please, and lead me to the truth."*

🍇

"I give myself completely to you, God.
Assign me to my place in your creation.
Let me suffer for you.
Give me the work you would have me do.
Give me many tasks, or have me step aside while you call others.
Put me forward to humble me.
Give me riches or let me live in poverty.
I freely give all that I am, all that I have, to you."

A METHODIST PRAYER

Principles *of* Pruning

The LORD will perfect that which concerns me;
Your mercy, O LORD, endures forever;
Do not forsake the works of Your hands.

PSALM 138:8

You've noticed that God never sends us a memo saying, "Pruning begins next Thursday at 3:15 P.M." He doesn't tell us what He'll do, how long it will last, or what methods He'll use. In fact, the whole process can seem mysterious until it's over and you can look back. David is a perfect example.

You remember the story in 1 Samuel 16. God told the prophet Samuel that he would find Israel's next king among the sons of Jesse. And right there, in front of a surprised family, David the shepherd boy was anointed as God's choice to succeed King Saul.

But before ruling came pruning. Years of it. The young prince had to fight a giant, fend off armies, and survive betrayal, loneliness, and assassination attempts. He spent years on the run, living in caves with his ragtag band of followers.

Had something gone terribly wrong? Not at all. God was using his trials to prepare David to be a king who would bear *much* fruit.

Pruning is always future-directed. No wonder pruning rarely makes complete sense to us at the time it's happening. We don't see results instantly; we just feel the shears. Not until the next season will we see God's purposes revealed—new fruit, new strength, and new beauty for Him.

Today I want you to consider several important principles of pruning:

- Pruning occurs when we're doing something right, not wrong.
- Pruning is initiated by God, not us, and is intended for our benefit.
- Pruning is custom-suited to one individual in a specific area of life.
- Pruning is applied only to a branch that is prepared to respond successfully.
- Pruning is usually applied indirectly through other people and circumstances.
- Pruning brings discomfort or stress, but if the branch cooperates, new levels of abundance result.
- Pruning is only as effective as we permit. Fighting against the process will eventually divert us back into fruitlessness and discipline.
- Pruning often goes on longer than we think is fair or necessary. Yet deep and repeated pruning *always* means a greater harvest ahead.

David submitted to it all. In the process, he learned about endurance, loyalty, leadership, submission to authority, dependence on God, and God's unfailing dependability.

David's prayers during these years, as recorded in the Psalms, are often full of honest searching. Yet he never wavered in his trust, even when he didn't understand God's ways. He wrote, "Because Your lovingkindness is better than life, my lips shall praise You" (Psalm 63:3).

Notice that David refused to believe the common heresy that says: "If God is happy with me, my life will go smoothly. If times are tough, God must be displeased or maybe just not paying attention." That lie stops God's work in our lives every time.

Have you prayed the Jabez prayer lately—for more blessing and influence so you can really make a difference for God—or pleaded to become more like Christ? Then your Father is pleased that you are following hard after Him...and you should get ready for pruning.

God isn't unhappy with you. Rather, He's delighted that you, like David, are a person after His own heart. You have an awesome future! And His perfect, loving plan is to prepare you for new opportunities to step up to your great destiny in Him.

My Vineyard Journal: *How can what I learned today change the way I think about certain ongoing events in my life?*

Those whose lives are filled with tragedy are not necessarily more sinful than those who seem to live in uninterrupted comfort. Job experienced calamity, not because he was wicked, but because he was righteous.

Erwin Lutzer

CROSSING *the* LINE

My brethren, count it all joy when you fall into various trials,
knowing that the testing of your faith produces patience.
But let patience have its perfect work,
that you may be perfect and complete, lacking nothing.

JAMES 1:2–4

James begins his letter with one of the most startling opening lines in Scripture—"Count it all joy when you fall into various trials."

Did he really mean to say joy? you wonder. *Wasn't he getting a little carried away?* But if you read the rest of his letter, you realize James is definitely not the bubbly sort. Like a battle-tested field sergeant, he's all business. And he means exactly what he says.

The "testing of your faith" that he writes about is simply another way of talking about pruning. And today I want you to consider what could possibly be joy-causing about such an uncomfortable process.

Remember that James wrote to Christians who had been severely persecuted and were now scattered across the Roman Empire. God was allowing them to be pushed to the very limit of their endurance…and then a little further.

Ever been there? Testings so intense they seem to cross the line of what's fair or even survivable?

At such times, we can feel like God has deserted us—or that if He's in control, then He's pushing too long and too far. Yet these are times of great promise. Our character and spiritual commitments are getting hammered out. As we come to the end of our power, we encounter the beginning of God's power. If we allow God to work, our faith will grow in ways we never thought possible. For first-century Christians, trials turned the raw ore of new belief into the steel of unshakable faith. And God used them to change the world.

I like to compare the faith-testing/faith-building process to what happens when you're weight training. Ken, a three-hundred-pound professional football player, gave me an inside perspective. "You train beyond what you can handle," he said. "Stress is what produces growth in muscle size and strength." For example, in the weight room, Ken bench presses to the point of exhaustion; then his spotter adds fifty pounds. At that point, Ken is no longer lifting what he can handle—he's resisting what he can't. "That's what it takes to build the strength I need to win," Ken told me matter-of-factly.

God sometimes grows our faith like that. After all, if we don't face new and even more difficult challenges, we don't need a greater level of faith. So God "pushes us" over the line. He allows circumstances to take us past what we can handle to teach us what God can handle through us. And our faith grows dramatically.

If you're like many believers I've talked to, you'll experience huge relief once you realize that God is not punishing you through trials, forsaking you, or even disciplining you! Your whole mode of thinking about tough times will get turned right side up. And you can open your heart for joy.

One day you'll look back on this test of your faith and see the wonderful changes it brought to you by God's grace. Not that you'd want to go through the test again, but you wouldn't trade what you've gained for anything. "Last week, Dominic and I suddenly noticed how far we've come in the last two years," a Montreal housewife told me recently. "It dawned on us when we realized that we think about money in very different ways now than we did before our financial crisis. Giving is such a pleasure now. We'd never go back to our old life!"

James didn't tell believers that they should put up with the pain of pruning, much less avoid it. He said to "count it all joy"! Why? Because God's objective in the test is to bless us with more faith, strength, and abundance until we become "perfect and complete, lacking nothing."

My Vineyard Journal: *When have I experienced a test of faith that eventually brought joy and other good results? Describe what happened.*

I owe more to the fire and the hammer
and the file than to anything else in my Lord's workshop.
CHARLES SPURGEON

STORIES *of the* KINGDOM

"But seek first the kingdom of God and His righteousness,
and all these things shall be added to you."

MATTHEW 6:33

Colleen had been praying for years that God would bring her husband a job that would allow him to stay home every night. Until she understood pruning, she spent most evenings idly watching TV or brooding. "I was miserable until I let God peel my fingers off what *I* wanted and accepted the opportunities He had been pressing on me—time with my kids, time for mentoring relationships with single women, time to seek Him. I'm still praying for a different job for Ed. But for all those years I missed out on the huge step forward in maturity that God had been wanting me to take."

Could it be that God's pruning shears are bringing you to a similar breakthrough? Colleen is in a much better position now to flourish, whatever her circumstances. And her marriage will be richer too.

I wish you could meet Harold, a property developer in the Southwest. For the last two decades, he's been leading a team that's turning thousands of acres of desert into a well-planned community.

"But that's only a half-time job," he says. He spends the other 50 percent of his time heading up mission projects around the world. "I've got a dream situation," he told me. "I get to do what I love to do and what God has gifted me to do to make a difference for eternity."

And I wish you could meet Luis, a friend who for the past fifty years has been giving one percent more to the Lord each year than he did the previous year. That would add up to a pretty high percentage by now, wouldn't it? Only a handful know about Luis's commitment. The last time I saw Luis, I asked him if things were getting tight yet. He laughed. "Bruce, I have more money now than ever before—and I'm having ten times the fun!"

Do you notice what these stories of the kingdom have in common? All are examples of a wholehearted and proactive response to the principles of pruning. These are people who have decided to "seek first" what God says should be first, and they're reaping a harvest in both personal fulfillment and ministry.

I've noticed that pruning changes us as God's branches in at least three tangible ways:

- We use our *time* differently.
- We use our *talents* differently.
- We use our *treasure* differently.

Consider where you think you have been during this past year in these three areas. Evaluate your level of proactive cooperation with God's priorities. Do you find evidence that still more fruitfulness for

God could be in your future? I certainly hope so.

When Jesus said that we should "seek first the kingdom of God and His righteousness," He was giving the first law of the truly abundant life. Throw all your energy into valuing what God values…and everything else that's worth having will come your way too.

MY VINEYARD JOURNAL: *"Heavenly Father, show me how, when, and where You want me to put Your Kingdom first in my life, and I will do it."*

Begin at once: Before you venture away from this quiet moment,
ask your King to take you wholly into his service;
then place all the hours of this day quite simply at his disposal and ask
him to make and keep you ready to do just exactly what he appoints.
Never mind about tomorrow; one day at a time is enough.
Try it today, and see if it is not a day of strange, almost curious peace,
so sweet that you will be only too thankful when tomorrow
comes to ask him to take it also.

FRANCES RIDLEY HAVERGAL

ARE YOU "OFF BALANCE"?

I also count all things loss for the excellence of the knowledge
of Christ Jesus my Lord, for whom I have suffered the loss of
all things, and count them as rubbish, that I may gain Christ....
One thing I do, forgetting those things which are behind and
reaching forward to those things which are ahead, I press toward
the goal for the prize of the upward call of God in Christ Jesus.

PHILIPPIANS 3:8, 13–14

When I was first learning about pruning, I made a point of asking Christian leaders I admired, "Have you been pruned much in your life?"

Without exception or hesitation, they would each say yes. Then they would slip into a reflective mood. Often, tears would come.

Now I understand. When God prunes, He reaches into the center of our being...and severs something. He cuts out a deeply-held assumption or value, a much-defended "inalienable right," a carefully protected priority or activity.

Pruning changes people.

Have you noticed? Well-pruned believers think differently about things. They carry themselves differently. They are so distinctively single-minded that they often seem oddly out of balance.

The truth is, most people I know who are extremely fruitful *are* "off balance" in the minds of men—and they don't want to get in balance! The pleasure of seeing God at work through them has become too pleasurable for them to want other pleasures. I've never heard one of these redirected Christians say, "Oh, I wish I could go back to the good old days." Instead, they look for ways to proactively participate in what God is doing. Like Olympic athletes, they're personally motivated to do all their coach asks and then some.

Today I encourage you to do the same. Here's an approach that has been helpful for me:

- Read through a year's worth of entries from your spiritual journal. If you haven't been keeping one, spend some time writing about your personal journey, especially about any struggles that show growth or a desire for it. Ask God to show you where He's trying to bring about change in your priorities or behavior.

- Write a statement (for each month, if possible) that shows what you've learned and denotes any major progress. Do you see strong evidence of having produced lasting fruitfulness for God? Or do your achievements show something less?

- Ask yourself, *What have I been doing that I no longer need to do? What less important thing do I do that someone else could do?*

- Identify the top three to five things (outside of your family commitments) that you do which have the most impact for God's kingdom. Ask yourself how you could rearrange your life to give more time to the top two than the bottom three.

- Set up a schedule for a daily, weekly, and quarterly pruning review. Ask, *What can I do now to cooperate with how God is trying to shape me for abundance?*

The best example in the New Testament of someone—apart from Jesus Christ—who chose to live "off balance" for God is the apostle Paul. During the course of his life, he set aside the pursuits of material comfort, safety, financial security, and public acclaim. It's as if on his journeys across the Roman world he discarded suitcase after suitcase of what had been good options. By the time he wrote his last letter, he was down to only one:

"One thing I do…I press toward the goal for the prize."

The only physical description we have of Paul comes from the second century: "He was a man of little stature, partly bald, with crooked legs…" But in today's passage, I see the real Paul. I see an Olympic runner, trained and focused and desperate for one thing: to break the tape. And he's streaking down the final stretch, straining to hurl his body first across the finish line. Maybe oddly off balance, but perfectly prepared to win!

My friend, as we close this week's study of pruning, I hope that you, too, fully embrace God's work of pruning in your life, believe His promise of greater things to come…and race for the prize.

MY VINEYARD JOURNAL: *The most important thing I learned about God this week was _____. The most helpful insight I learned about pruning was _____.*

Do you not know that those who run
in a race all run, but one receives the prize?
Run in such a way that you may obtain it.
And everyone who competes for the prize is temperate in all things.
Now they do it to obtain a perishable crown,
but we for an imperishable crown.

1 CORINTHIANS 9:24–25

Week Four

FLOURISHING *in*

HIS PRESENCE

*My soul waits for the Lord
More than those who watch for the morning.*

PSALM 130:6

THE QUIET MIRACLE

"Abide in Me, and I in you.
As the branch cannot bear fruit of itself,
unless it abides in the vine, neither can you,
unless you abide in Me."

JOHN 15:4

It was our third night at a fishing lodge above Lake Clark in western Alaska. Six men playing in paradise: pulling salmon from icy streams by day, eating hearty meals around a campfire by night. That kind of life can get even the most cautious man to open up.

On the third night, Arlen did. "Guess I ought to tell you guys I'm planning to resign when I get back home," he said, staring into the fire. For the last thirty years, Arlen had been a music and worship leader in his denomination. But while his programs were running better than ever, Arlen was running dry. "I told my wife it's time to get honest," he continued. "I love God. I want to serve Him more than ever. But not enough is coming back anymore. I'm working harder and enjoying it less. I don't know what to do except step aside."

Readers of *Secrets of the Vine* will know that I came to a similar crisis years ago. Like Arlen, I felt confused and exhausted. Like Arlen, I felt I was trying harder only to hit a wall of defeat and discontent. Yet that crisis turned out to be a doorway, not a wall—a threshold to a new and higher level of fruitfulness for God.

If you recognize your spiritual experience in this crisis, I have good news for you: *God has brought you to this place and time.* Your dissatisfaction is a gift from God to prepare you for what comes next. And what comes next is an invitation….

Let's take another, more careful look at the vineyard. In every vineyard a season comes when nothing happens…or so it seems. The cleaning and tying up is done. The pruning shears are put away. Luscious clusters of grapes crowd the well-tended branches.

Nothing happening? Don't miss the invisible miracle! It's the sap that surges up unseen from earth to roots, roots to vine, vine to branch, branch to fruit. Jesus had this unseen river of life in mind when He said, "Abide in Me, and I in you. As the branch cannot bear fruit of itself, unless it abides in the vine, neither can you, unless you abide in Me."

Abiding happens at the exact place where the branch touches the vine. The larger the union between vine and branch, the more sap can flow, and the greater the potential harvest. In the same way, through a shared connection that Jesus called abiding, God pours His life into ours.

Arlen and I simply needed to pursue and guard our union with God with as much energy as we had invested in serving Him. The irony for us is that our push for fruit had gotten ahead of our intake of sap. We needed to grow in abiding, to radically enlarge our capacity to take in God's river of life…and we needed to do it fast.

In the preceding three weeks, we've talked about how much God wants more fruit—good works—from our lives and what actions He takes to help it happen. This week we discover the third secret of the vine: *If your life bears a lot of fruit, God will invite you to abide more deeply with Him, the result of which will be much fruit.*

The best miracle of the vineyard is invisible, but what it produces is not. Amazingly enough, it's only as we accept His invitation to genuine intimacy with Him that we can reach the highest levels of fruitfulness possible.

That night around the campfire, Arlen's confession prompted a vigorous and candid conversation about the perils and extraordinary promise of the season of abiding. Arlen went home with an unusual assignment: to do less *for* God and to be more *with* Him. I'm happy to tell you it was the beginning of more fruitfulness—and more fulfillment—in his family, marriage, and ministry than he ever thought possible.

MY VINEYARD JOURNAL: *How does the idea of doing less so that I can spend more time with God appeal to me? How could that possibly lead to more fruit?*

God cannot give us happiness and peace apart from himself,
because it is not there. There is no such thing.

C. S. LEWIS

CLOSE *the* DISTANCE

"Let him who glories glory in this,
That he understands and knows Me."

JEREMIAH 9:24

The Fosters were neighbors who became part of our family. I still remember their tiny two-story house in New Jersey. Aunt Belle baked the world's best apple pies; Uncle Sherman loved to watch the Yankees on TV. I grew up thinking that their marriage and their home was the picture of coziness—until one day, long after they'd both passed away, when my dad told me they had been...well, strangers.

"Did you ever see the Fosters eating at the same table or talking together in the same room?" Dad asked. It dawned on me that I hadn't. Dad explained.

One day after work, Sherman had been in such a rush to get upstairs to watch a baseball game that he'd forgotten to take off his muddy boots. When he came down for dinner, the floor had been cleaned but the table was set for only one. Belle stayed in the parlor. The next morning, Sherman came down for eggs and toast, but still no Belle. After several weeks of this, Sherman left a note on the table: "If you want to see me, just tap the pipes." But Belle never tapped the pipes.

"How long did that go on?" I asked Dad.

Seventeen years, he said—until the day Aunt Belle died.

Can you imagine living with another person in the same house for that long without speaking? How tragic! But this story reminds me that as Christians we can spend years of our lives in close proximity to God yet live as strangers. We can ignore Him, push Him away, or simply fail to try. And the results are always heart-breaking.

The wonderful promise of abiding is that an invigorating friendship with God is both possible *and* expected. In fact, the Bible teaches that the depth of our friendship with God should be one of the most important criteria for how we measure true achievement. "Let him who glories glory in this," God told Jeremiah, "that he understands and knows Me" (Jeremiah 9:24).

As you look back over your Christian experience, do you sense a growing familiarity with God? Or do you see something less? Take a few minutes today to inventory the quality of your friendship with God. Check the category which comes closest to describing your current level of intimacy with God.

____ *Aloof.* You feel somewhat distant or even indifferent. God generally exists outside of your range of daily concerns. You know more *about* Him than you know Him as a Person.

____ *Acquaintance.* You try to pray and "check in with God" from time to time, especially if you're facing trials. Several times in your Christian experience, you have felt close to God.

____ *Associate.* Your relationship is mostly a working partnership. You pray and obey in exchange for His help and involvement in your life. You try to treat God with respect, and you sense His concern.

____ *Affectionate.* You are getting to know Jesus as a Friend. Your heart is involved; you like and appreciate His character and His role in your life. When your spiritual life falters, you miss Him.

____ *Abiding.* A daily awareness of God is your greatest joy. You hide nothing from Him because you trust Him completely. You serve Him with affection and passion. His goals and your goals are becoming more the same.

How do you feel about your conclusions? I urge you to take this little exercise to heart. Your spiritual fulfillment and your personal fruitfulness are at stake. And God's heart is on the line.

Ever since Eden, God's dream has been communion with His children. Throughout history, He has pursued friendship and reconciliation with humans. "All the dealings of God with the soul of the believer are in order to bring it into oneness with Himself," wrote Hannah Whitehall Smith.

Today the God of the universe wants to enjoy your company. Don't let another day pass in which you live like strangers. Ask Him to show you what steps you can take to close the distance in the most important relationship of your life.

MY VINEYARD JOURNAL: *"Lord, how amazing it is to think that You care so much about being close to me! You are always near to me; please show me how to be near to You today."*

&

Human fellowship can go to great lengths but not all of the way.
Fellowship with God can go to all lengths.

OSWALD CHAMBERS

To have found God and still to pursue Him
is the soul's paradox of love,
scorned indeed by the too-easily-satisfied religionist,
but justified in happy existence by the
children of the burning heart.

A. W. TOZER

The Person You Seek

"As the branch cannot bear fruit of itself,
unless it abides in the vine,
neither can you, unless you abide in Me."

John 15:4

One person in the New Testament seemed to understand abiding intuitively. Her name was Mary. Along with her sister Martha and brother Lazarus, Mary lived in Bethany, a village near Jerusalem. The three—who apparently lived together without spouses or children—held a special place in Jesus' heart. John reports, "Now Jesus loved Martha and her sister and Lazarus" (John 11:5).

When Jesus and His disciples stopped at their home one day, Martha made the perfectly responsible "ministry" choice. She threw her energies and skills into making sure everyone was cared for. But Mary chose something else. Luke writes, "Mary...sat at Jesus' feet and heard His word. But Martha was distracted with much serving" (Luke 10:39–40).

Try to absorb the elements of this scene: an important visitor, clusters of hungry guests, Martha scurrying to meet needs. But in the middle of that bustle and clatter, one person sits at Jesus' feet—

watching, listening, enjoying His presence.

Mary chose to abide. And when Martha asked Jesus to rebuke her sister for not caring enough to serve Him, Jesus said He couldn't. Why? Because Mary had chosen to be *with* Him, and that was the best choice.

It's easy for us to confuse abiding with some kind of mushy, mystical state. But Jesus wants us to see abiding first in physical terms:

- A sturdy vine surging with sap and a branch sprouting from it—and at the place where they join, an unseen river of life coursing through.
- Eleven men leaning close by lamplight so they don't miss a word from their Lord and Friend.
- A woman surrounded by hubbub and pulled at by a hundred duties—but sitting still, listening, looking up into the face of God.

The little vignette of that home in Bethany illustrates a number of principles of abiding.

Abiding is with a Person, not a program or doctrine. We don't have to wait for a religious service or special program to abide. Mary made it a priority to sit at Jesus' feet. She set aside time for Him, risked criticism for Him, and gave His words her full attention. Every action and priority was focused on spending time with Jesus.

Abiding with Christ is available to any believer at any time or place. The family in Bethany had to wait to see Jesus until He came to their village. But we have the indwelling God with us at all times (John

14:16–17). We can abide no matter what our age or level of spiritual maturity. We can abide in a traffic jam, a doctor's office, or a laundry room. Abiding has nothing to do with our denomination, temperament, family background, education, or any special ability.

Abiding has no limit of depth or length. Even though Jesus was a frequent houseguest, Mary didn't assume she was as close to the Master as she could get. Like the connection between vine and branch, our capacity for relationship with God can keep expanding. A. W. Tozer wrote, "A vessel that grows as it is filled will never be full. The soul is like that. The more it wants, the more it is given. The more it receives, the more it grows."

Abiding must be pursued to be enjoyed. Abiding doesn't come naturally; there will always be "more important" distractions—even the distraction of serving God. That's why Jesus *commanded* His disciples to abide. We should read His imperative to mean, "I already abide in you—now you must choose to abide in Me."

Do you face seemingly insurmountable obstacles to abiding? Remember Mary's choice, the circumstances in which it happened, and the favor it brought her. Remember Susannah Wesley. A busy mother of more than a dozen boisterous kids (John and Charles among them), Susannah found a way to abide. Whenever she put a bag over her head, every Wesley child knew not to interrupt— Mother was spending time with God. And the fruit from Susannah Wesley's life (she's one of the most important figures in revival history) is still being counted.

Maybe today you should go looking for an old grocery bag!

MY VINEYARD JOURNAL: *Think of what your best friend (outside of marriage) does that makes—and keeps—your relationship so important to you. Ask how you could demonstrate your friendship to God in similar ways today.*

We are called to an everlasting preoccupation with God.

A. W. TOZER

That which we have seen and heard we declare to you,
that you also may have fellowship with us;
and truly our fellowship is with the Father
and with His Son Jesus Christ.

1 JOHN 1:3

"ABIDE *in* MY LOVE"

"As the Father loved Me,
I also have loved you; abide in My love."

JOHN 15:9

Sharon, a reader of *Secrets of the Vine,* wrote to say she was particularly struck with the statement that Christians don't abide with God because they don't believe He likes them.

"How sad, and how true!" she wrote. "I see God as someone disappointed in me and 'unpleasable' instead of someone who really enjoys my company."

Sharon is not alone. Countless Christians carry around the millstone of imagining an untrustworthy, unlikable God. You might be one. You might assume God loves you—after all, loving the world is His job. But deep down, you suspect God doesn't really *like* you. Fixing you? Sure. Saving you, too. But spending time in your presence, enjoying the real you? That's difficult to imagine. "He knows everything I've done!" you wail. "How could He be interested in my company?"

What words would you choose to describe God's attitude toward you? Take a moment to circle the numbers on the following scale that most accurately describe how you feel today.

I think of God as:

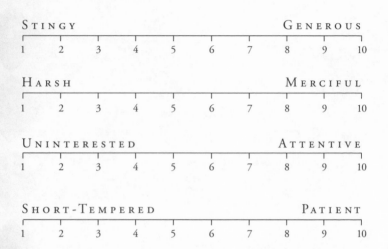

STINGY   GENEROUS
1   2   3   4   5   6   7   8   9   10

HARSH   MERCIFUL
1   2   3   4   5   6   7   8   9   10

UNINTERESTED   ATTENTIVE
1   2   3   4   5   6   7   8   9   10

SHORT-TEMPERED   PATIENT
1   2   3   4   5   6   7   8   9   10

If all or most of your choices fall toward the right side of the scale, you have an accurate picture of God. How do I know? Because when Moses, who spent great amounts of time in God's presence, asked God to show him His glory, God delivered a stunning self-portrait. He described Himself as "merciful and gracious, longsuffering, and abounding in goodness and truth" (Exodus 34:6).

If, however, all or most of your choices fall toward the left side of the scale, you identify with Sharon. Therefore, pursuing a deeper familiarity with God may not seem possible or desirable to you.

I assure you that God wants the truth about Him to change how you think. Once you know God for who He is, the horizons of abiding will open before you.

Put yourself in the following story:

Suppose you're on your third week of setting aside time to abide with God. Things could hardly be going worse. You've missed more morning appointments than you've kept. Last night before you went to bed you got into a shouting match with your teenager. You got so rattled that you stepped outside to smoke a cigarette, a habit you thought you'd finally licked six months ago.

This morning you've slept late. Pressed for time, feeling resentful, and without brushing your teeth, you stumble into your study to grab your Bible when…

You notice an angel seated in your chair! His face is aglow, and his whole being shines with a beautiful, holy radiance.

"Wha…what are you doing here?" you gasp.

"I'm supposed to meet God here now," the angel says calmly. "I have a morning appointment with Him."

"But…so do I," you reply….

This fanciful story leads to my question: Assuming God could keep only one appointment this morning, whom would He choose to meet with—you or the angel?

My friend, there's no contest. God would choose you over the angel in a heartbeat. Unlike any angel, you were created by God in His image with friendship specifically in mind. He knows everything about you—the beautiful and the blotchy—and He loves you. Furthermore, there are no conditions on His love because He *is* love! (1 John 4:16).

Here's another truth you may find shocking: God wants to abide with you more than you want to abide with Him. When He spun the strands of your DNA in the secret rooms of eternity, He had no one but you in mind. He made you—just you—on purpose, with pure delight, and with great anticipation. There's nothing you could do that would change His mind about sending Jesus to die for you. And today He longs for the pleasure of your company.

I hope you keep your appointment.

MY VINEYARD JOURNAL: *What incorrect idea about God has kept the most distance between us? What would God want to say to me today about that idea?*

How precious also are Your thoughts to me, O God!
How great is the sum of them!
If I should count them,
they would be more in number than the sand.

PSALM 139:17–18

Believe God is always the God you know Him to be
when you are nearest to Him.

OSWALD CHAMBERS

Beyond Simple Disciplines

As the deer pants for the water brooks,
So pants my soul for You, O God.
My soul thirsts for God, for the living God.
When shall I come and appear before God?

Psalm 42:1–2

As a young man, I remember setting off for seminary, determined to get the secrets of the Christian life nailed down. By the time I attended my first chapel I was already outfitted for religious success, armed with a brand-new Hebrew Old Testament, a Greek New Testament, and a briefcase full of theology books.

When the president of the seminary, Dr. John Walvoord, announced his topic—"The Secrets of the Spiritual Life"—I couldn't believe my good fortune. Here I was, not even a week into training, and the president was already going to tell me exactly what I'd come to find out.

Dr. Walvoord proceeded directly to his outline. "There are three secrets," he said. I hurriedly pushed "record" on my tape machine. Then he unveiled the secrets: *Read the Bible every day. Pray all the time. And share your faith with everyone who doesn't know Christ.*

My heart sank. Why, I'd been hearing those "secrets" in church since I was a kid!

Yet looking back now on Dr. Walvoord's advice, I see that he was absolutely right. In our quest to know God better, it's practicing the basics that yields results.

You've probably already heard the secrets of abiding too. But I wonder—have you decided to make them a necessary part of your life?

Let me suggest three steps that may seem simple but are absolutely necessary if you want to break through to abiding:

1. Plan your devotional time. Set aside a time when you are at your freshest. Morning is best. Find a comfortable, completely private place and go there every day. Most of us can't add one priority without giving up another, so decide what you will let go.

2. Practice the primary spiritual disciplines. Even though abiding doesn't mean working harder, it is still our responsibility. Abiding is not passive; it is something we choose to do. Here are the essentials:

- *Read the Bible.* God's Word is your primary resource. Receive it as His living letter to you. If you feel stuck, start with Psalms and Proverbs, then add a Gospel or an Epistle. Don't worry about how much you cover; just read until your mind and heart open to the Word.

- *Pray.* Begin with a one- or two-sentence prayer in your journal. Pray out loud if it helps you stay focused. Keep track of God's answers. Practice honesty, respect, and careful listening. You're talking to a Person, and this is the most important conversation of your life.

- *Praise.* Express your thankfulness and worship to God. Praise enlarges your trust in God, invites joy, and trains your heart to hope.
- *Keep a spiritual journal.* Write down what you're learning, which Bible verses you want to remember, and what you want to tell God. Measure your spiritual progress with an occasional review of your journal. It is a record of a living relationship.
- *Fast.* In fasting, you present your deeply-felt need to God as an act of worship and faith, asking Him to fill you up. Even a brief fast can add more sensitivity to your spirit and more life to your praying.

These practices take effort (that's why they're called disciplines). But simple as they are, they can bring lasting change for you as they have done for generations of pilgrims. Whether you're eighteen or seventy-eight, they can reshape your life so dramatically that you'll soon be living at a level of fruitfulness and fulfillment that you assume is impossible now.

Yet shockingly, you can do every discipline for years without abiding. Many Christians do. These are methods; abiding is a dynamic relationship with a Person. These are observable actions; abiding is an invisible awakening.

That's why my third suggestion may be the most important of all:

3. Pursue God with all your heart, determining that you will seek Him until you find Him. If you do this, I promise you'll begin to abide. I can say that because God guarantees it. "Draw near to God and He will draw near to you," the Bible says (James 4:8).

"You will seek Me and find Me, when you search for me with all your heart" (Jeremiah 29:13).

The very fact that you are reading this page means that you deeply desire to be near to God. Your spirit thirsts for Him, like the deer panting for water in today's verse. Go in earnest search of God today—and never stop.

If you make your move, He'll make His.

MY VINEYARD JOURNAL: *How would I describe my devotional practices to a close friend? Which one area would God most want to see growth in?*

When You said, "Seek My face,"
My heart said to You, "Your face, LORD, I will seek."
PSALM 27:8

Lord, I do not know what to ask of you;
only you know what I need. I simply present myself to you;
I open my heart to you.
I have no other desire than to accomplish your will.
Teach me to pray. Amen.
FRANÇOIS FÉNELON

THE MEASURE *of* FRIENDSHIP

The Lord is near to all who call upon Him,
To all who call upon Him in truth.

PSALM 145:18

Y ou'd recognize Mariana right away. She's that pretty young
mother we all know who has struggled with her weight ever
since she started having babies.

Darlene met her at a weekend church retreat. Over grapefruit
one morning, Mariana listed the diet plans she'd tried. She had just
quit on number seventeen. "The diets probably work," she told my
wife. "It's me that doesn't work. I fall off the wagon, put the pounds
back on.... Why even start again?"

Maybe you identify with Mariana's defeat when you think about
the spiritual discipline of abiding. So many have told me that their
efforts to get up early to spend time with God don't last more than a
couple of weeks. "I'm convinced I'm actually an Egyptian," a Chinese
student told me once with a big grin. He explained that every New
Year's he resolves to read his Bible through, starting at Genesis 1. But
his reading plan always seems to go down to defeat by the time he gets
to the story of Pharaoh's army drowning in the Red Sea (Exodus 14).

If abiding is an invitation from a loving Father, if it is a *command,* and if it is the only way to experience the very best the Christian life has to offer, why do so few of us manage to succeed?

Based on what I've heard from hundreds of Christians, I've concluded that one of the most common roadblocks to abiding seems to be this: We measure our success by feelings, and we depend on them to keep us motivated. For example, we assume that if we're abiding, we will feel a deep intimacy, a warm glow or rush of excitement, a powerful conviction that we are connecting with God. When we feel little or nothing we decide we're not abiding. Then, rather than face more guilt and failure, we quit.

Yet we know that emotional responses are determined by many factors—our physical condition, how much sleep we've had, whether we're anxious or depressed, how much coffee we've consumed, the weather, our basic temperament type. In fact, we don't judge our marriages and other significant friendships on feelings alone. No wonder that gauging intimacy with God by feelings alone quickly gets us in trouble.

One kind of trouble is that we focus on manufacturing the missing feelings. Over the last twenty-five years, there's been a tremendous movement in the church that places a top priority on feelings. Your emotions, some would say, determine whether you're truly worshiping, when you're close to God, and when He's leading you.

Unfortunately, too many Christians go home from enjoying an emotionally charged worship service only to slip into a lifestyle the rest of the week that disregards, offends, and dishonors God. They got the feelings, all right, but they didn't find the Person. Yet the Bible is clear: "If we say that we have fellowship with Him, and walk in darkness, we lie and do not practice the truth" (1 John 1:6).

Ultimately, your decision to abide is a gift of faith you present to God with sincere desire and respect—faith, because you believe what He says; desire, because you value His presence and the fruitfulness He promises more than any immediate sensation; respect, because you know relationships just don't get anywhere without it.

Thankfully, emotion *is* a wonderful part of a genuine spiritual experience. Those feelings of exaltation and release matter to God. Yet He is equally committed to your whole person—mind, heart, body, soul, and spirit—and He invites all of you into the adventure of knowing Him.

If you identify with Mariana's reluctance to start abiding again, I have good news: You don't need more Bible reading and prayer; you need to reach for God Himself.

Pull up a couple of chairs. Someone is waiting outside who wants very much to meet you. And this is His message to you today and every day: "Behold, I stand at the door and knock. If anyone hears My voice and opens the door, I will come in to him and dine with him, and he with Me" (Revelation 3:20).

His knock comes again at the door of your heart. Do you want Him to come in for a visit? Then just open the door and welcome Him.

MY VINEYARD JOURNAL: *How have I misunderstood the role of emotion in my relationship with the Lord? How might my times of abiding change if I were to stop measuring their success by my feelings?*

People who live in their emotions do not always see this.
They feel so at one with Christ that they look no
further than this feeling and often delude themselves
with thinking they've come into divine union when
all the while their nature and dispositions
are still under the sway of self-love.

HANNAH WHITEHALL SMITH

You will seek Me and find Me,
when you search for Me with all your heart.

JEREMIAH 29:13

"EXCEEDINGLY ABUNDANTLY ABOVE"

To know the love of Christ which passes knowledge;
that you may be filled with all the fullness of God.
Now to Him who is able to do exceedingly abundantly
above all that we ask or think,
according to the power that works in us.

EPHESIANS 3:19–20

Perhaps a man who has been an ordained minister since 1914 ought to be ashamed to confess that he never felt the joy of complete surrender," wrote Frank Laubach in 1930. By then he'd been a missionary in the Philippines for years. But after being seized by what he called "a profound dissatisfaction," he decided to try to consciously live every waking moment in God's presence.

Most friends told him it couldn't be done, but Laubach was determined. To give focus to his abiding, Laubach ordered his days by the question, "Father, what do You desire *this minute?*" To Laubach, that seemed to be how Jesus lived.

The experience changed his life. After several months of his new spiritual exercise, Laubach wrote in his journal: "I think more clearly. I forget less frequently. Things which I did with a strain before I now do easily and with no effort. I worry about nothing. I lose no sleep. I walk on air a good part of the time. Even the mirror reveals a new light in my eyes."

Have you experienced similar benefits from abiding? Today I want you to see that God wants to bless you by His amazing presence at all times.

Laubach discovered an aspect of abiding that is often missed. The word *abide* is also translated "remain" or "stay." Too many of us leave God in the study or beside our favorite chair after we've completed our devotional time. But the lessons of the vine show us that we were created for *unbroken* abiding. We can "stay" even as we go.

Brother Lawrence called this dimension of fellowship "practicing the presence of God." As Laubach found, when we pursue Him with this kind of intensity and persistence, we see astonishing and very tangible benefits. For example:

Unbroken abiding renews us in body, heart, and spirit. How quickly we forget that to do God's work we need God's presence and power! The more experience we have, the easier it is to coast along on our talents or track record. But like Arlen, whom we met earlier this week, we eventually learn we can't coast forever without rolling to a stop.

Continual abiding prevents burnout because we're constantly being refueled. Think of the sap of a vine branch as the power and energy of the Holy Spirit. When we stay connected to the Vine, we are "renewed day by day" (2 Corinthians 4:16).

Unbroken abiding increases our spiritual discernment. Paul told believers to "let the word of Christ dwell in you richly" (Colossians 3:16). That kind of enrichment takes time. When we abide with Christ, we understand His will more profoundly. Wrote Laubach, "The sense of being led by an unseen hand which takes mine while another hand reaches ahead and prepares the way, grows upon me daily."

Unbroken abiding changes us on the inside. We've all noticed how couples who've been married for years begin to talk alike, think alike, even look alike. The Bible says "He who walks with the wise grows wise" (Proverbs 13:20, NIV). So it is when we spend a great deal of time abiding with Christ. We are transformed more to His likeness, and in His newness our ministry becomes more powerful and effective.

Unbroken abiding changes the way we pray—and God answers! Consider this astounding promise: "If you abide in Me…ask what you desire, and it shall be done," said Jesus (John 15:7). Twice in the same chapter Jesus made this promise in relation to abiding (vv. 7, 16). Why?

When we have surrendered ourselves to God, our requests are much more likely to reflect His desires. Have you ever noticed that the majority of miracles in the New Testament happen in the middle of ministry? That's because our prayers have the most power when His will and our will have become most nearly one.

Do you begin to see it? Maximum fruitfulness is the result of ongoing, unbroken abiding with Christ because He is the source of all eternal good anyway.

As we close this week on experiencing God more deeply, I hope you are tasting the pleasures of God's company in new ways and already seeing new fruit in unexpected places. My prayer for you is that you will "know the love of Christ which passes knowledge; that you may be filled with all the fullness of God" (Ephesians 3:19).

God wants you to be filled with His fullness today. And He is able to do "exceedingly abundantly above" all you can ask or imagine (v. 20).

MY VINEYARD JOURNAL: *Choose to turn your thoughts to God every fifteen minutes all day long. Write down verses, tips, or reminders that can help you accomplish your goal.*

Moment by moment I'm kept in His love;
Moment by moment I've life from above;
Looking to Jesus till glory doth shine;
Moment by moment, O Lord, I am Thine.
DANIEL W. WHITTLE

Epilogue

THE PRIZE of
ABUNDANCE

*The joy our Lord experienced came from
doing what the Father sent Him to do.
And He says to us, "As the Father has sent Me,
I also send you."*

OSWALD CHAMBERS

WISDOM *of the* SEASONS

Therefore be patient, brethren, until the coming of the Lord.
See how the farmer waits for the precious fruit of the earth,
waiting patiently for it until it receives the early and latter rain.
You also be patient. Establish your hearts,
for the coming of the Lord is at hand.

JAMES 5:7–8

If you've ever been a parent, you can probably remember the first time you realized things were turning out all wrong. I remember when our first child turned from a sweet baby into a screaming two-year-old. After he had thrown a tantrum for the third time in one meal, Darlene and I were in shock. What had we done wrong?

We went scrambling to parenting books for help. Maybe if we could intervene immediately, we wouldn't have a lifelong disaster on our hands.

But we quickly discovered that our son was fine. In fact, he was right on track and doing his noisy best to be a good two-year-old. Our expectations were fine too. We just needed to adjust them to our son's season of growth.

It's the same in God's vineyard. Change for any of us is nearly always difficult, often not very pretty, and usually takes more time than we'd like. That's why we shouldn't expect to see an immediate link between what God is doing to our branch and big results. Did you know that grape plantings in California's Napa Valley often don't reach peak productivity for fifty years? Fruitfulness takes time. Maximum abundance usually takes a lifetime.

Seasonal wisdom doesn't necessarily mean that the older we are in Christ, the more fruit we will bear (we've all seen fifty-year-olds behaving like children). But it does mean that the more mature we become in Christ—as a result of cooperating with the Vinedresser—the greater our capacity to bear fruit will be.

In the graph that follows, you'll see time charted horizontally and the intensity of the particular season charted vertically. Take a minute to study this graph of how the seasons of discipline, pruning, and abiding change throughout our lives. It is based on biblical principles, my own personal experience, and the experiences of thousands of other believers.

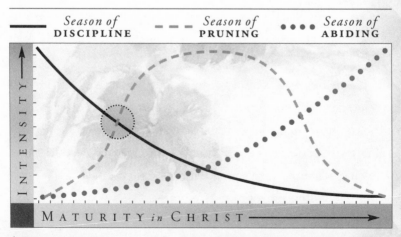

A COMPARISON OF COMMON PROGRESSION THROUGH THE SEASONS

What does this graph show? First, notice the shape of discipline. It is most intense early, and it falls steadily into maturity, where it becomes minimal but not absent. Now look at the course of pruning. It is a bell-shaped curve, progressing from a light amount at the beginning, reaching its most intense in midlife, and then receding. Finally, notice that the intensity of abiding is nearly the mirror opposite of discipline—it is least significant early on (though always present), and it rises steadily in later years with no limit in sight.

Does this picture of the seasons in the vineyard correspond with your understanding of Scripture, your observation of others, and your own experience? Where would you place yourself on this graph right now?

If you're at or near the point where the lines of discipline and pruning first intersect (the dotted circle), you're in a particularly important and vulnerable time. The seasons are changing in and around you. The weather can be turbulent, and you can easily misread the signs (of course, Satan wants you to). But it's also a time of great promise, and what you've learned in this book and in *Secrets of the Vine* will help you respond appropriately to God's work in your life.

No matter what season you're in today, you can reach for and receive great encouragement. Your Father doesn't expect you to instantly reach maturity or to make your transition to more fruitfulness with perfect grace and style. Instead He takes great delight in watching you grow. Like any loving parent, God can always see past your present limits to your future promise.

MY VINEYARD JOURNAL: *Based on where I think I am now (according to today's chart), what changes should I expect in the near future? In what ways could I prepare now for greater fruitfulness later?*

"The sower sows the word.
But these are the ones sown on good ground,
those who hear the word, accept it,
and bear fruit: some thirtyfold, some sixty,
and some a hundred."

MARK 4:14, 20

SECRETS FOR CHURCHES

"As many as I love, I rebuke and chasten.
Therefore be zealous and repent.
Behold, I stand at the door and knock.
If anyone hears My voice and opens the door,
I will come in to him and dine with him, and he with Me."

REVELATION 3:19–20

I'll never forget the Sunday morning I watched a large church congregation "wake up" to their specific season in the vineyard— and to what God wanted them to do about it.

I had been asked to preach in both morning services (the church was temporarily without a pastor). Things went well until the middle of the second service, when God seemed to bring me up short. I felt compelled to stop and switch directions.

"I sense that the Spirit of God is quenched in this service," I explained to the startled audience. "Something is wrong. Am I correct?"

A long pause. Then heads began to nod in agreement. Finally people started speaking up. They told me they had recently gone through a painful split. Members had left angry. Many who had stayed were holding onto deep resentments. As they talked, I discovered that this was the first time the church had spoken openly about their problem.

"If you want the Spirit of the Lord to flourish here, you need to face the sins that are separating you from God's best," I told them. Then I asked, "Do you want to flourish?"

When nearly everyone said yes, God's hand was released to move in a remarkable way. Hundreds came forward to pray and weep and then to ask forgiveness of each other for injuries done. When the service seemed to be complete, I said, "Friends, I sense that the Spirit of God now dwells among us with great pleasure. What do you feel?" People spontaneously started to applaud.

The service I just described marked the end of discipline and the beginning of new fruitfulness for God for that church and in that community. If the congregation hadn't faced their sin and repented, they could have endured intensifying discipline for years (probably blaming the next pastor for their continuing blight).

Up until now, our conversations about Jesus' teachings have focused on individuals. But as this story demonstrates, the principles of the vineyard apply to groups too—families, churches, Christian businesses, and ministry organizations. Think of such groups as rows of grapevines or even as whole vineyards. Today I want you to take this wider view.

Let's look at three New Testament churches. In Christ's message to the churches of Revelation, we clearly see that each body was primarily in one of the three seasons. For example:

1. *The church at Thyatira was in discipline (and heading for scourging).* This group had followed false teachers to lead members into serious sin. Christ sent them a stern message: "I gave her time to repent…and she did not repent. Indeed I will cast her into a sickbed, and those who commit adultery with her into great tribulation, unless they repent of their deeds" (Revelation 2:21–22).

2. *The church at Smyrna was in pruning.* The believers there were about to be tested. Their calling was to endure. "I know your works, tribulation, and poverty (but you are rich)…. Do not fear any of those things which you are about to suffer…. Be faithful until death, and I will give you the crown of life" (Revelation 2:9–10).

3. *The church at Philadelphia was ready to abide.* This church received neither a rebuke nor an exhortation like the other churches, only an invitation: "Behold, I stand at the door and knock. If anyone hears My voice and opens the door, I will come in to him and dine with him, and he with Me" (Revelation 3:20).

Have you ever considered that your church or Christian organization could be in discipline, pruning, or abiding? Take a moment to apply what we've learned over the last four weeks. (You might find it helpful to refer to the appendix on page 124.) Which season in the vineyard do you think your church might primarily be experiencing right now?

Whatever you do, don't become critical and judgmental of your church, using labels instead of love. But understanding how God may be at work in your church will give you and those you fellowship with insights about how to respond to Him. You'll know better how to pray and where to apply your energies. Together you'll have a clearer sense of how to respond for maximum spiritual blessing and abundance.

MY VINEYARD JOURNAL: *"Lord, show me how You're working in my family, business, or church today. Show how I can help. And grant me the discretion and humility to serve You well."*

Christianity is an individual thing,
but it is not only an individual thing....
The local church or Christian group should be right,
but it should also be beautiful.
The local group should be the example of the supernatural.

FRANCIS SCHAEFFER

We...do not cease to pray for you,
and to ask that you may be filled with
the knowledge of His will in all wisdom
and spiritual understanding;
that you may have a walk worthy of the Lord,
fully pleasing Him, being fruitful in every good work
and increasing in the knowledge of God.

COLOSSIANS 1:9–10

THE FACE *of* FRUITFULNESS

"This is my commandment, that you
love one another as I have loved you.
Greater love has no one than this,
than to lay down one's life for his friends."

JOHN 15:12–13

I've never met Amy, but she holds a special place in my heart. She's a wife and the mother of two kids from Florida who attended one of my seminars on fruitfulness several years ago. Recently I received a letter from her that I want to share with you.

That weekend when I heard you speak [Amy's letter begins], I was struggling with my dependence on alcohol. For years I justified my habit, pointing out to my husband and even my two small kids that it wasn't wrong to drink—even every day—unless I got *drunk*. When I attended your seminar, I knew God was convicting me of sin in this area. But I resisted.

Just as you predicted, God wasn't going to give up. Finally the pain in my life drove me to my knees, and I attended my first accountability group in the basement of a local church. It was there that I met Shelly. She was single and lonely. We began to get together for coffee after the meetings. Soon it became obvious that Shelly was searching for God. Hesitantly, I began to talk to her about Jesus. Every time I said His name, her eyes welled with tears. Finally one night she asked me to pray the prayer of salvation with her.

Amy's letter went on to explain that in the coming year she watched Shelly begin a Christian singles' study that grew into a vital ministry. But when Shelly relocated, the two lost touch. Her letter continued:

> Then one morning as I drank my coffee and read the paper, a name caught my eye and stuck there. The name was Shelly's. The date was yesterday. The age was hers. And so was the accident. Shelly had died instantly when a truck hit her car head-on.
>
> Even as my tears splashed on the newsprint, I knew without a doubt that Shelly was safe in God's arms. And in the days that followed—including Shelly's memorial service, attended by over five hundred people—bearing fruit took on a whole new meaning for me. I kept thinking, *What if I hadn't responded to God's discipline?* Now I feel such an intense urgency to produce a harvest for God. I'll never look at my life in the same way again.

My friend, it is exactly this kind of urgency that I hope you experience today. I believe Jesus felt it that night in the vineyard. Our Savior knew that death waited for Him just around the corner. But first there were things that needed to be said—memorable word pictures, secrets of the vine.

Notice how Jesus concluded His sermon on fruit bearing. He put it in very human terms: "This is my commandment, that you love one another as I have loved you. Greater love has no one than this, than to lay down one's life for his friends." Then He went willingly to the cross, because He loved us more than His own life.

That's what it takes to bear eternal fruit. We are called to die every day—to sin, to personal rights, to self—and then to reach with all our might for the new life God offers.

Are you willing, my friend?

When you leave this book, I want you to remember the lessons of the vineyard and the metaphor of fruitfulness. But when you stand before your Father in heaven, you probably won't see a single grape! Instead you'll see faces. Your "fruit" will crowd around you, smiling and nodding. They are people you took one step closer to Christ. They are the ones who blossomed because of your words and deeds. Some would not be there were it not for your singular passion to be fruitful for God's glory....

And the Vinedresser will say, "Well done, good and faithful servant!"

Jesus talked about grapes to show how God works in our lives and what He wants most from us. Jesus wanted us to know what really counts in this life. Every word of this devotional has been intended to give you a clearer sense of what really counts—and to help you pour your life into exactly that *right now.*

I hope you never look at your life the same again.

MY VINEYARD JOURNAL: *What do you remember most about the lessons on fruit bearing from Jesus' teachings in the vineyard? What could you do to keep them fresh in your memory and in your walk with God?*

For this reason we…ask that you may be filled with the knowledge
of His will in all wisdom and spiritual understanding;
that you may walk worthy of the Lord, fully pleasing Him,
being fruitful in every good work and increasing in the knowledge of God.

COLOSSIANS 1:9–10

THREE SEASONS
in GOD'S VINEYARD

DISTINCTIVE ISSUES	THE SEASON OF DISCIPLINE	THE SEASON OF PRUNING	THE SEASON OF ABIDING
YOUR MAIN ARENA OF GROWTH	Sin	Self	Savior
GOD'S MAIN OBJECTIVE FOR YOU	Purify your behavior	Prioritize your values	Pursue your relationship with Him
WHAT GOD WANTS MOST FROM YOU	Obedience—to stop your sinning	Trust—to drop your distractions	Love—to deepen your friendship
WHAT YOUR BEST RESPONSE WOULD BE	Repentance	Relinquishment	Relationship
WHAT YOU SHOULD SAY WHEN YOR PRAY	*"Help me, Lord! Forgive me and deliver me from sin."*	*"Use me, Lord! Change me so I can do more for you."*	*"Draw me closer to You, Lord! Nothing else really matters but You!"*
WHAT YOU WILL EXPERIENCE	Restoration	Release	Rest
WHEN THIS SEASON WILL END	It ends when you stop the sin	It ends when you change your priorities	It doesn't have to end (God wants it to go on forever!)
WHAT GOD WANTS MOST TO GIVE YOU	Fruit from an obedient life	More fruit from a pruned life	Much fruit from an abiding life

PLEASE BE SURE TO VISIT US AT
www.secretsofthevine.com

The BreakThrough Series, Book One
The Prayer of Jabez™

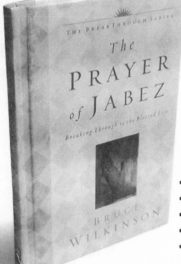

#1 *New York Times* Bestseller

11 Million In Print!

- ISBN 1-57673-733-0
- 11 Million in Print!
- www.prayerofjabez.com
- www.jabezmillion.com
- 2001 Gold Medallion Book of the Year

The BreakThrough Series, Book Two
Secrets of the Vine™

#2 New York Times Bestseller

- ISBN 1-57673-975-9
- Over 3 Million in Print!
- www.prayerofjabez.com
- www.jabezmillion.com

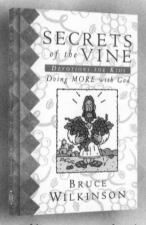